PSYCHOLOGY IN THE CLASSROOM

UNIVERSITY OF

Also available from Cassell:

Mark Fox: *Psychological Perspectives in Education*
Dennis Child: *Psychology and the Teacher*, Fifth Edition

Psychology in the Classroom
Reconstructing Teachers and Learners

Phillida Salmon

CASSELL

Cassell
Wellington House
125 Strand
London WC2R 0BB

215 Park Avenue South
New York
NY 10003

First published in 1988 as *Psychology for Teachers: An Alternative Approach.*
British Library Cataloguing-in-Publication Data
A catalogue record for this book is available from the British Library.

ISBN 0–304–33254–2 (Hardback)
    0–304–33256–9 (Paperback)

Printed and bound in Great Britain by Biddles Ltd, Guildford and King's Lynn

Typeset by Create Publishing Services Ltd, Bath

Contents

Acknowledgements

The previous version of this book, *Psychology for Teachers*, greatly benefited from the generous support of Margaret Meek.

More recently, I have found inspiration in the work of Jean Jones and her colleagues in initial teacher education at the London Institute of Education. Hilary Claire has been a valuable resource, and Sheila Macrae has offered helpful criticism. Leon Gore and Veronica Nevard have provided vital advice on particular topics. Ann Phoenix responded to the manuscript with characteristic insight and encouragement.

I could not have written the book without the personal support of Noel Byass.

Introduction

Can there be a case for yet another book on the psychology of education? With the mountain of such books already on the shelves, have psychologists anything new to say? At the present, critical time for teachers, the voice of George Kelly, as yet barely heard, is surely worth listening to. For this psychologist, though he wrote his main work in 1955 and died only a decade later, offers an approach to learning and education which effectively opposes today's dominant ideology.

Kelly labelled his psychology 'personal construct theory'. These terms define his fundamental assumption; that each of us can know the world, and engage with it, only through our own network of personal interpretations. In this philosophy, we do not just carry meanings in our heads; we actually live out these meanings in our lives. In some sense we *are* our constructs.

This psychological approach was born at a time when a basically mechanistic approach, that of behaviourism, was dominant. In education, as elsewhere, emphasis lay on externals: on historical and circumstantial causes of personal difference, on the control of behaviour, and learning, by reinforcement. For those who encountered it, Kelly's philosophy came as a breath of new, refreshing air. But these encounters were exceptional, happening through personal acquaintance with the enthusiasm and brilliance of Don Bannister, who made the dissemination of this philosophy his life's main work.

Don Bannister's own commitment to personal construct psychology (as it is now known) was rooted in his large-scale work on schizophrenic thought disorder. Discovering Kelly's two-volume tome in the course of an exhaustive library search, he saw within it a revolutionary approach to this clinical problem. No human condition could have entailed a tougher challenge. In the consensus of the day, schizophrenic thought-disorder had been relegated to psychological incomprehensibility; a meaningless by-product of psychopathology. Yet by exploring the networks of meaning, the personal construct systems, of thought-disordered schizophrenics, Bannister revealed that their symptoms made sense. In a Kellyan perspective this condition emerged as meaningful, not meaningless.

For all the excitement which this approach generated in those who came across it, personal construct psychology, at least in education, has remained relatively obscure. This is certainly due in part to the clinical rather than educational contexts in which it has typically been adopted. But to some extent, the forms in which Kelly's ideas have usually been presented have also acted to distance, if not actually alienate, those who might have found them congenial. Kelly's two-volume formulation of his approach is highly formal, even abstruse. The first volume presents a 'fundamental postulate' and 'eleven corollaries'. The second illustrates these with reference to clinical applications. For present-day readers, the use of sexist language throughout the book represents a further barrier.

Sexist language is also inevitably present in a further book *Clinical Psychology and Personality: The Collected Papers of George Kelly* (1969). It is from this book that many of the quotations within the present volume are taken. It comprises a number of papers, collected after his death by Brendan Maher, in which Kelly evidently felt free to express his ideas in much more informal ways. Eloquent, funny and personal, these essays convey, far better than his formal exposition, the essential spirit of this approach.

Personal construct psychology is also expounded, in an accessible way, in a book which Bannister wrote together with Fay Fransella: *Inquiring Man: The Psychology of Personal Constructs* (1986). This has had deservedly wide circulation, and is now in its third edition. But its brief is a broad and general one, and educational concerns have only a small place in it. This is not to say that others have not applied Kelly's ideas to issues of learning and teaching.

More than a decade ago, Maureen Pope insisted on the relevance of this approach to initial teacher education (Pope and Keen, 1981.) More recently, Laurie Thomas and Sheila Harri-Augstein have developed Kelly's repertory grid methods to devise ingenious forms of self-organized learning. Their book *Learning Conversations* (Harri-

Augstein and Thomas, 1991) describes their own distinctive modes in guiding self-directed kinds of learning. As a practising educational psychologist, Tom Ravenette has also pioneered a variety of Kelly-inspired, informal approaches to problematic learning situations. Unfortunately this work is as yet unavailable in print.

None of these books are written specifically for teachers. Yet teachers, of all practitioners, seem likely to find Kelly's ideas meaningful and supportive. This book seeks to present his approach in relation to the actual situation in which teachers are now working. In struggling to maintain their own professional integrity within the present hostile and alienating climate, teachers may, it is hoped, find in these ideas encouragement and inspiration.

Chapter 1

The Schooling Enterprise

It might simplify matters if we could set up a system of monetary exchange under which each of us could translate his dependencies into terms of money. Then with our pockets full of loose change we could put a coin into the slot whenever we saw something we wanted. Some people. I am sure, think this is what civilization amounts to, or what maturity means. Why barter for anything: just buy it! To get what you want, you first exchange your services for money. You may have to sacrifice some of your independence, but you will acquire power, and power is what it takes to get anything in this world. Any kind of perceptive giving – giving affection, offering sensitive support to some-one in trouble at a timely moment, or personifying the fulfilment of another's hopes – if these acts do not fit into the economic scheme, they are old-fashioned and a waste of time.
(*Maher, 1969, pp. 200–1*)

During the course of 1994 every household in the UK received an attractively illustrated pamphlet, sent by the Department of Education. This was the Parents' Charter. It offered a guarantee to parents: a guarantee of their rights and entitlements as the consumers of educational provision. For underpinning the recent and unprecedented interference in schooling has been the metaphor of education as a supermarket. And in this metaphor, parents, as buyers, possess a pre-eminent place. It is for them that the merchandise of education is to be set out on display. And if they are to exercise their entitlement – to purchase for their children the best learning that is on offer – they must shop around, and from the diversity of schools available, select their own options.

Followed through to its ultimate conclusion, where would the logic of market forces take schooling? Pupils, like their parents, would be consumers, but in a much more literal sense: obediently swallowing the dishes set before them. And if children could not work on what they got, or shape for themselves the material of their learning, neither to any significant extent would teachers be doing so. For the products of education would be ready-made; all packaged up, labelled, and set out on the supermarket shelf. Teachers would be merely the purveyors of these goods. Well-trained shop assistants, they would know the prices of their merchandise, could point out the whereabouts of the stock, and reach up helpfully for inaccessible items.

At the centre of these imaginary transactions between parents, pupils and teachers, would stand the goods; learning and education. In this philosophy, these would not be processes but products – products made parent-proof, pupil-proof and teacher-proof. As they filled up their shopping trolleys, parents could, of course, pick only from the selection on display. Nor for children, as pupils, could personal diversity affect what they received; everyone would get the exactly the same package. The product would be bland, uniform and homogeneous, the alternative brand labels disguising only marginal differences.

Who would decide what should constitute the commodities in this educational market? Ostensibly it would be a simple matter of market forces, of supply and demand, of provision arising out of the choices made by individuals. Yet some customers would be more equal than others. The range of items on the shelves might adequately meet the wishes of some social groups, but there are others whose needs would not be catered for. A tiny section of the shop might perhaps offer a few constituents for Greek Cypriot, Korean or Afro-Caribbean cooking, and might provide a handful of organically grown veg-etables and a pack or two of humanely reared meat. But ethnic or cultural minorities would have little influence on the stocking of the supermarket shelves. Just like the ideal Sainsbury shopper, the proto-type buyer of educational provision would be white, affluent, and a subscriber to traditional values.

In the operation of the educational market, there would of course be an unseen player in the cast, a hidden hand manipulating the action. Behind the rhetoric of market forces, of competition, account-ability, choice and diversity in education, lie certain vested interests; interests which parallel those of the multinational companies and agribusiness empires in the supermarket world. For this market would certainly also be rigged. To the present political hegemony, a genuinely open educational system, responsive to the needs and wishes of all its members, would constitute a fundamental threat. Only by extending an ever-tightening control throughout the whole structure of schooling could dominant social and political interests be protected.

The barrage of recent legislation, the endless stream of new initiatives and directives, represent a co-ordinated attempt to translate this metaphor into educational reality. Government determination to control schooling – to convert the system into one version of market forces – has resulted in a massive reorganization. Little has remained untouched. Schools, colleges, universities; their structures, functions and ways of working, their relations with funding and administrative bodies, have all been radically altered. The constitution of the schools' inspectorate on the one hand, of governing bodies on the other, have alike been remade. Parents have been accorded a new and prominent status. The organization of pupil groups is once again to be geared, wherever possible, to selective principles. Pedagogy itself is under official scrutiny, with pressures towards didactic and whole-class teaching.

Nor has the teaching profession remained outside the ambit of centralized control. Government intervention has reached into initial teacher education, into the definition and appraisal of professional competence. It has entailed a reconstitution of the roles of heads and deputies, and ramified in multiple direct and indirect ways into teachers' classroom work. Even the professional relations between schools and between colleagues have been subject to political manipulation. League tables, incentive schemes, performance related pay, all act to introduce professional rivalry and insecurity, and undermine social solidarity.

On the bed of Procrustes to which an authoritarian government has tried to fit the education system, the real goals of learning and of teaching would be very ill-served. Equality of access, that much-vaunted market principle enshrined in the Parents' Charter, could only be an empty slogan while basic social inequalities remain. In choosing from the inevitable hierarchy of schools, some parents would be winners, others losers. For the more privileged, superior access to information would enable better choices, while their own improved resources would mean resource reduction for poorer schools.

Where pupils are concerned, a market system would more likely shut down than open up learning opportunities. Of course academically able children, particularly if middle class, would find their own way through the system, qualifying themselves for a successful adult life. But for the majority, schooling would certainly prove increasingly inaccessible. Within the constraints of the narrowly prescribed and Eurocentric curriculum dictated by the dominant political constituency, ethnic and cultural minorities would see few reflections of themselves and their lives; it would be hard to engage with school learning. Difficult, disruptive children, children with 'special needs': these pupils would face a still more serious predicament. In a system of compulsory competition, no school could afford to house threats to all-important league tables; resort to exclusion would become ever more frequent.

Pupils and their parents look generally diminished rather than enhanced in this model of education. How does its rhetoric portray teachers? For those who have chosen to enter this profession, the market metaphor – at least in its most blatant form – holds up a distorting mirror in which they can scarcely recognize themselves. Reduced to deliverers of a ready-made product, they find their professional autonomy and judgement, their hard-won special expertise, virtually passed over.

Government intervention within the initial education and conditions of employment for teachers has already gone some way towards undermining professional integrity. In legislation to remove initial training from institutes of higher education, there are direct threats to the complex reflective and conceptual work involved in preparation for teaching. And by the moves to employ minimally qualified assistants, professional practice is implicity defined as a simple catalogue of easily acquired practical skills.

The market model reduces human transactions to buying and selling, and translates human values into those of commerce and economics. In this metaphor, schools are essentially businesses, with head teachers appointed to run them. Humane educational concerns – to create a learning community in which every child is acknowledged and enriched, every colleague respected – such concerns can have at best only the most marginal place within an enterprise in which economic efficiency and accountability are the real goals.

Head teachers, caught up in Local Management of Schools, must in this version of education also carry reponsibilities for advertising.

The school world is now supposed to be one of cut-throat competition; competition for funding, for resources, for very existence. Survival is to depend on effective public relations. In an attractively designed pamphlet aimed, like a holiday brochure, to catch its clientele, every possible selling point must be cleverly packaged up, every potential drawback skilfully glossed over.

Teachers work at the chalk face of a system under siege. Many of their problems are far from new. But not merely do they go unresolved within the dominant educational ideology; they are implicitly denied, airily passed over in the hectic, remorselessly positive language of the market. School buildings are often very old, their physical fabric seriously decaying. Most suffer chronic shortages of space and equipment. Books that are both out of date and in short supply are typical at primary as well as secondary level. In many schools, staffing levels are quite inadequate. Yet the need for central funding which could remedy these problems is altogether bypassed in a rhetoric that makes schools responsible for their own economic viability, and blithely presupposes uniformly affluent local communities, able to offer unlimited financial support.

Difficult and disruptive children, challenges to teachers' authority, the ever-present threats to classroom order: these problems are not new either, even if the number of disaffected pupils is likely to have grown. There is a personal cost in the constant containment of these situations, in the maintenance, day after day, of a calm and benign atmosphere. For most teachers, teaching is never altogether without tension, never entirely stress-free. But nothing of this is acknowledged in the language of the market, which has no place for human relations other than those of commerce. Its perspective on classroom problems and their resolution is that of management. Hostile, stressful relationships are merely the result of planning failure, of inadequate managerial strategies, of poor time management or ineffective reward systems.

The market model fails to concede, let alone actually address, many problems that are all too familiar to today's teachers. But perhaps still more seriously, at every level of the profession it has tried to impose its own new, impossibly heavy burdens. While frequently submerging teaching staff under a mountain of administrative, pedagogic, assessment and curricular directives, it has at the same time often deprived them of vital professional support. Isolated and overworked, teachers are struggling to maintain their contact time with pupils, amidst the ever-growing load of paperwork – of increased marking and preparation, of additional, essentially bureaucratic tasks, of multiple official and informal meetings – work which increasingly takes over precious personal time, evenings, weekends and holidays.

Metaphors are powerful things. The model of the market does not merely put its own gloss on established educational practice. It channels and constrains the whole enterprise of schooling. As the currently dominant educational ideology, this metaphor has, at least to some extent, forced the institutions and practitioners of education into the culture, the roles, the modes of commercial undertakings. In the process it has attempted to reduce the rich and complex stuff of human learning to a prescribed series of unproblematic givens.

Yet of course this model has not entirely won the day. So crass, so simple a formulation could hardly hope to defeat the professionalism of teachers themselves – their dedication, ingenuity, resourcefulness and sheer determination. The essential weakness of a market forces metaphor in education lies in the dismal poverty of its conception. In its image, the content of schooling becomes just a shelf-full of tins and packages. Yet for those who teach, the material of classroom learning represents a world of human possibility and potential inspiration. It is in the sphere of the school curriculum that the market model has been most strongly contested. And in the course of this struggle, teachers have succeeded in regaining vital educational ground.

In the reconstruction of the educational curriculum, politicians no doubt saw an opportunity to bring schooling more closely under centralized control. But in the event, the wholesale rethinking of the materials of school learning – the reflection on underlying concepts and assumptions, the recasting of the complete curriculum in thought-out and coherent form – has proved a major vehicle through which to counter simplistic thinking and arbitrary practices in education.

During the prolonged work that has led to the National Curriculum in its present form, the whole framework of school learning has been comprehensively put at issue. In the process, ideas about knowledge and understanding have been clarified, with classroom work being closely considered in relation to them. The outcome, for most subjects, has been the development of a more disciplined and more focused approach to learning. The notion of learning as a process rather than merely a product has gained ground, transforming some subjects. In science, for instance, the emphasis on experimentation and investigation builds in the importance of personal meaning.

Perhaps nowhere is this general enlightenment more evident than in the redefinition of history. Previous work at primary level, for instance, sometimes demanded the unthinking regurgitation of facts. But existing orders insist that history means actively interpreting evidence, working with chronology and sequence, and, in understanding the past, acknowledging a variety of perspectives.

The National Curriculum, as it has now been achieved, offers teachers a professional framework within which to reflect on their own classroom practices. It embodies a serious attempt to redefine school learning as an intellectual progression to which every child is entitled. For all its current overload, its over-prescriptiveness of some areas, in recasting the National Curriculum the educational profession has surely succeeded in subverting political attempts at curricular manipulation.

But if teachers have, at least in part, defeated reactionary and authoritarian directions in the sphere of the curriculum, this has not enabled the schooling system at large to escape the pernicious influence of a market forces model of education. For as long as this model remains generally dominant, efforts to reform schooling can remain only piecemeal. This book is an invitation to view the enterprise of schooling in very different terms. Against the intellectual poverty, the mean-spiritedness of the market image, personal construct psychology offers a largeness and generosity of conception. Its philosophy of learning is one in which teachers themselves may find some of their own deepest values, their own richest meanings.

In the dominant ideology, education is a privatized and acquisitive affair. Only at the checkout need the supermarket shopper have any human dealings at all, and these are of the most routine and minimal kind. The purpose of shopping, after all, is individual possession; learners are to pack away their own selection of educational commodities for their own personal use. Yet the exchange and extension of human meaning, which the process of education must in the end represent, is surely nothing if not a matter of social and cultural engagement.

The social and cultural character of knowledge is fundamental in George Kelly's psychology of personal constructs. Even our understanding of the physical world is derived from concerns and undertakings whose purpose and meaning are socially and culturally relative. Science, as Werner Heisenberg (1958) proclaimed, does not tell us about nature as such; rather, it gives us answers to our questions about nature. What we observe is not raw reality, but reality as exposed to our methods of questioning it. Differing cultures, differing societies; each sees life in its own distinctive way. In every historical era, there have been different burning issues. The questions we ask of nature are rooted, finally, in our particular human culture.

In this philosophy, social commonality and mutuality are basic to the human enterprise. Our constructions of the world are deeply embedded in our social identities and engagements. They carry our shared values, they inspire and underpin our collective endeavours. But of course human society is not all of a piece. Inequality and oppression act to ensure differences in the sense which people make of their worlds. There are many social realities, competing and conflicting meanings which struggle with each other. Diversity of values is not to be reduced to the different brands of baked beans.

The educational enterprise cannot afford to ignore the social constitution of human understanding. Teaching, in the portrayal of the market model, involves the offer of wares that are ready-made and universally desirable. To a Kellyan, this will not do. Teachers, as themselves members of socio-cultural groupings, bring to classrooms their own particular meanings, their values, assumptions and taken-for-granted realities. Yet in their teaching, they meet and must engage with the perhaps very different meaning-worlds of pupils. In building bridges, they may come to create new kinds of understanding.

In the metaphor of market forces, learning, like shopping, is an occasional activity: one in which learners invest little of their own vital selves. But for Kelly, learning, in its largest sense, is the very stuff of living. 'All behaviour is an experiment', he remarks. Every human engagement, every relationship, every personal undertaking, carries its own kind of question. It is on the outcomes of these endeavours that we build extensions to our personal understandings, and venture our next commitments. For human learning, in this understanding of it, is not a dry-as-dust collection of abstractions, but the whole network of intuitive meaning from which we actually live.

This approach also carries a very different perspective on educational content. Knowledge can never be final. As Kelly suggests: 'The world is open to an infinite number of constructions, and many of the best ones have yet to be devised' (Kelly, 1955, p. 12). Though school knowledge may represent the best so far, it remains essentially provisional, open to contest and redefinition. Market goods pose no problems; they just sit there, all wrapped up, their reality beyond question. But in Kellyan psychology the curriculum is never closed, understanding never reaches a full stop. Everything is always open to reconstruction; in this human race, no one ever gets to the end. To some people, perhaps, this might seem a depressing picture. Not to Kelly.

> The living history of man is the story of the questions he has enacted rather than the conclusions he has anchored in science or dogma. Finding the ultimate explanation of something is about the same kind of quest as trying to capture certainty in a formula, or truth in a bucket. Besides, I am not sure most of us would care to be dragged, kicking and screaming, through life by its certainties, or to have our burning curiosities extinguished by being doused with a bucketful of truth. ...
> A world jam-packed with lead-pipe certainties, dictionary definitives and doomsday finalities strikes me as a pretty gloomy place.
> (*Maher, 1969, p. 43*)

Personal construct psychology does not separate learning from learners and their personal situations and predicaments. George Kelly was himself a life-long psychotherapist. His views were forged out of daily contact with men and women struggling to remake difficult lives. Such origins have acted to ensure a keen awareness of the sheer difficulty of the learning enterprise. Real learning – learning that makes a difference – is seldom simple or easy. We may have to abandon precious assumptions, move away from the safety and comfort of what we have always thought we knew. Human change, when it is significant, can be hard, risky and costly.

The image of education offered by the metaphor now dominant is depressingly limited. Though consumerism has its own pleasures, the reduction of the whole human quest for understanding to the routine of a visit to the supermarket makes it into something dull and familiar. This is very unlike a Kellyan picture. However difficult, however problematic, learning in this model does not look dull.

This book sets out to examine the implications of personal construct psychology for some of the vital issues entailed in the enterprise of schooling. For each of these issues, its perspective is very different from that which sees education as fitting into a simple market economy.

Ideas about schooling derive most basically from assumptions as to the nature of education. What sort of a process is it? What does 'being educated', in both senses, actually mean? What part do learners and teachers essentially play in the process of education, and how do their roles need to mesh together? Chapter 2 is concerned with these kinds of question.

For a market forces model, the process of education is straightforward and unproblematic. You pays your money and you takes your choice. The range of goods is on display; all purchasers need do is survey the selection and make their choice. Leafing through the advertising brochures of competing schools, parents consider the various possibilities. This school offers a well-equipped science laboratory, but that one has large playing fields and an emphasis on sport. Then there is that other school, further away but with the best exam results.

Probably for many people, this picture would ring true. Parents do of necessity make choices such as these, deliberating with great care, often with great anxiety, weighing up possible assets against possible deficiencies in their children's school futures. But difficult though such decisions may be, they involve a familiar and unambiguous activity; the exercise of personal preference within a range of possible options. For this model translates the process of education into a set of clearly definable products: the educational equivalent of a row of alternative branded goods. Parents are seen, not as merely choosing the context within which their children will engage in educational ventures, but as directly buying education. This is because the market metaphor short-circuits the whole complex business of schooling, making it into something simply defined and easily deliverable to purchasers.

Such a view could hardly be more different from a Kellyan one. For Kelly, education is above all a matter of enquiry. And it is the questions, rather than the answers, which count most. A set of answers might, perhaps, be translated into the kind of currency in which a market model deals. But in this philosophy learning proceeds by refusing to settle for what is already known; by personally setting things at issue and following where the outcomes lead. As many teachers would themselves testify, classroom work carries significance when it takes off from pupils' real questions.

A model of education which accords the highest value to human questioning must necessarily view learning and teaching in process rather than in product terms. So far from being specificable in advance, as marketable goods, the outcomes of any educational endeavour are by definition unknown at its start. And this is not the only fundamental difference between the two approaches. They contrast equally in their view of learners and teachers.

In the model of market forces, learners and teachers have the two complementary roles of consumers and purveyors; teachers provide, pupils consume. The transaction is guaranteed by its purchase on the part of parents. When it is over – when the goods have been exchanged and consumed – teachers and pupils leave the scene, to resume their lives, perhaps as purchasers, purveyors or consumers of other kinds of goods. They go from the classroom essentially unchanged, as the same people they were when they entered it. But in Kellyan psychology, real education is not so easily divested; learning leaves its mark. For better or for worse, we ourselves are changed by the enquiries we undertake.

Chapter 3 considers teachers and teaching. Though teachers are often neglected in books about school learning, their part in the enterprise of education is no less complex than that of learners. Of course this is not apparent within a market model, which reduces teaching to the mere purveying of existing commodities. The relation, in this image, of teachers to their curriculum is entirely impersonal. A good salesperson can move without difficulty from one department to another in the store: yesterday selling shoes; today, covering for a sick colleague, in cosmetics. To the salesperson it makes little difference; the same presentational routine, the same well-practised approach to customers serve equally well in both spheres.

For Kellyan psychology, with its stress on personal meaning, this kind of separation cannot hold. What two teachers make of the same English syllabus is not, as any pupil would confirm, the same thing. In teaching, we offer something of the real inner meaning which the lesson material has for us. It is the sense of richness, or, conversely, of secret emptiness which, as teachers, we convey. Because in teaching we actually represent, stand for, the material we offer, our personal position towards it is far from incidental.

If you are merely selling goods, your personal characteristics do not really matter. So long as you conform to respectable norms of dress and manner, and follow the usual sales procedures, you will be able to perform your role successfully. But as a Kellyan teacher, you cannot possibly remain so unremarkeble. Your personal, social, cultural identity are inextricably involved in your classroom work. To pupils, the person of their teacher, and the stance which that teacher takes towards them, carry messages which, in countless subtle and implicit ways, facilitate or undermine possibilities for learning. And for teachers, an understanding of all this forms an essential aspect of their own professional expertise.

Schools, as institutes of learning, form the focus of Chapter 4. Both approaches would accord significance to this feature of education. For a market model, the setting matters. Like any successful department store, a school would need to be designed so as to attract consumers, and maximize the selling power of its commodities. A pleasant and comfortable environment, which puts its customers at their ease, making them receptive to the persuasiveness of the goods on display: that would be the aim. If newly opted-out schools characteristically commit their extra funding to features which enhance the attractiveness of their own environments – rather than to extra staffing for instance – this is perfectly in line with the philosophy which underlies their existence.

For a Kellyan approach, the significance of schools is very different. In this philosophy institutions are not just physical buildings, but sites of culture, with their own distinctive social practices. At one level, this calls for close attention to the multiple, typically implicit ways of doing things that have been labelled 'the hidden curriculum'. Many of these contain messages that are at odds with official educational policy, for instance, messages of exclusion for minority group pupils. No less profoundly important are the cultures which pupils themselves bring to school, and elaborate within its world. For it is these which govern, not just the interrelationships of young people, but ultimately their position towards school learning.

The necessity to engage with pupils' own social and cultural realities applies equally, in Kellyan philosophy, to the content of classroom work, curriculum material itself. This is the topic of Chapter 5 in this book. If schooling is merely a matter of meeting the demands of customers, there is nothing very complicated about it. The education system has only to offer a range of available kinds of curriculum to purchasers, and supply those that are most widely chosen.

Personal construct psychology makes meaning central. One implication of this is that, to some extent, the material of learning must be constantly recreated. It cannot, therefore, be nailed down in advance. Learning, if it happens, does so through the engagement of living concerns and understandings on the part of learners. Classroom work has to meet, to make room for pupils' often diverse realities. Educational material which bypasses the experience, the street wisdom, of young people in classrooms cannot hope to make an impact on the sense they make of the world and of their own lives. This necessarily calls for a certain kind of flexibility in the content of school work. Only if the National Curriculum avoids over-prescriptiveness may it stand a chance of achieving its own ambitious educational goals.

It is perhaps on the next topic (in Chapter 6), that of the learning process itself, that these two philosophies of education look most starkly different. Again, the market metaphor paints a simple picture. Its image of consumption has pupils unproblematically taking in, absorbing, whatever is presented to them. A Kellyan approach depicts another scene altogether; one which in its complexity would be far more easily recognizable to teachers themselves.

If personal meaning is the anchor of new learning, it is also undoubtedly its stumbling block. For all the new things that we may learn in our lives, there are probably very many more that we fail to learn. Simple exposure to 'facts' is no guarantee of their absorption. What is learned must be assimilable with what is already known. Most fundamentally, this means that new knowledge must fit with the sense of personal identity. Testing out such personal implications is a vital part of learning. This means that learners need a kind of protected space in which they can inwardly try things out, without as yet 'owning' their new knowledge.

Nor is learning, as a rule, the easy and painless process of consumption that the market model makes it. All new understandings involve, to varying degrees, a sense of confusion, perhaps even of disorientation. The learning process may bring exhilaration, but it is also likely to entail discomfort at some stage. Its progress is in any case typically bumpy and erratic. So far from being a simple additive progression, the acquisition of new meaning is a wayward process, full of false starts and blind alleys.

Chapter 7 is concerned with pupils who are defined as 'special'. For a market model of education, the position of pupils who do not fit narrowly defined norms is dire. In the world of the market, the majority is king. Those who, by force of numbers, can afford consumption on a grand scale, can dictate what commodities shall be put on sale. Commercially insignificant, the wishes of small minorities are of no concern to suppliers: such consumers must buy what is on offer, or go without.

What would this mean in schooling terms? Unlike the large conception which originally inspired the term 'special need', the definition of pupil difference would carry clear connotations of lesser, of inferior. To the extent that this metaphor prevails in the organization of schooling, the consequences of this attitude are already visible. The imposition of league tables as the officially validated index of a school's worth has led to a quiet abandonment of integration. Fearful of an image which might frighten off prospective parents, some schools have even dismantled their own successful special units.

In personal construct psychology, the concept of 'normal' has little meaning. Within its philosophy, every human being is genuinely unique. In engaging with their pupils, schools and teachers need to address and respect their distinctive personal identities. Given the deeply rooted institutional structures and practices of schooling, this is of course far easier said than done.

A Kellyan approach has no room for the constitution of difference as deviance, and its consequence in ignoring or demeaning those who become so labelled. What does this approach offer hard-pressed teachers struggling to cope with classroom members who require constant attention, who disrupt lessons or persistently fail to learn? Personal construct psychology has no panacea for dealing with exceptionally difficult pupils. But its approach is one which informs and supports teachers in their insistence on continuing to treat even the most troublesome children in human terms.

Kelly argues for an abandonment of what he calls the language of complaint. Faced with a pupil who is behaving impossibly, it is difficult not to resort to such language; to label him or her 'disturbed', a child with serious behavioural difficulties. While this may bring a kind of solution – his or her removal from the class, perhaps the school – it fails to resolve the classroom impasse in which pupil and teacher have become enmeshed. Instead of focusing on the unacceptable consequences of a pupil's behaviour, so runs Kelly's logic, we need to explore what that behaviour means for the pupil, what he or she is trying to achieve by it. Hostility always represents a desperate bid to stave off a deeply threatening situation. Looking at behaviour in this way may sometimes allow a different kind of enagement.

The last chapter in this book takes as its subject the professional learning of teachers themselves. How does this look if we see education as a market? Certainly this is a topic of some concern to those who promote such a view. Government initiatives in initial teacher education bear witness to this interest. As one would expect from those who view schooling as a matter of buying and selling, the preparatory learning of teachers is to be cut severely down to size. If teaching is merely a matter of purveying ready-made goods, then teachers have no need for all the thinking, the discussion of social and moral issues, the sustained reflection on their own practice which have formed the basis of initial education up to now.

On this view, learning to teach means acquiring a simple range of practical skills. Further professional education is just a matter of updating these skills, when there is a change in the educational commodities themselves, or when a particular new skill becomes needed. Such an approach could hardly be more unlike that of Kelly. For personal construct psychology, the learning of teachers is no less complex than that of their pupils.

The approach advocated in this book does not divorce learning or teaching from the personal, social and cultural identities of those involved. This means that teachers' learning, whether at initial or subsequent stages, must integrate concerns about their professional practice with their own personal values and commitments. Classroom skills or curricular materials are not to be objectified, depersonalized or considered apart from those who deal in them. Just as pupils need to reconcile new understandings with their sense of themselves, so the particular teaching stances demanded in new professional initiatives have to fit with teachers' own convictions.

The demand for professional learning frequently comes from outside, and as such, may bypass teachers' own felt needs, or fail to fit with particular classroom realities. However well intentioned, such initiatives all too often fail to take. In contrast, professional development that is undertaken by teachers themselves, working collectively, may achieve usable kinds of good practice. When this happens, it is likely to be due, not only to the personal commitment of those involved, but also to the fact that consideration can be given to the social and cultural character of particular institutional settings. No teacher is an island. School ethos, the head, colleagues, staff room culture; these crucial features surround individual practitioners, constraining or facilitating what may be professionally possible.

As an educational approach, personal construct psychology leads in directions diametrically opposed to those of a market forces model. It emphasizes the complexities of teaching and learning, and on no aspect of the schooling enterprise does it offer easy answers. But fundamentally, this approach is inspired by a sense of the human value of learning, of the ultimate worth for human progress of brave and committed enquiry into the unknown. In this, the Kellyan conception of education surely echoes the ideals of teachers themselves.

Chapter 2

Kellyan Education

> Learning is not a special class of psychological processes: it is syn-
> onymous with all psychological processes. It is not something that
> happens to a person on occasion: it is what makes him a person in the
> first place.
> (*Kelly, 1955, p. 303*)

At the age of 14, alone among my classmates, I took up the option to
study Latin. Over two years for three periods a week, I had individual
lessons with an elderly woman teacher. In the eccentric independent
school I attended, this teacher was one of the few members of staff
who had stayed more than a couple of terms. Her main subject was
scripture, as it was then called. By the time I made my choice to study
Latin with her, I knew this teacher very well. To the whole group of
my contemporaries, she was a figure of fun, laughed at for her
old-fashioned clothes and pedantic manner, cruelly compared with
the vital and glamourous young women teachers who passed briefly
through the school. Scripture, her subject, was held in very low
esteem. The lessons were occasions in which we vied with one another
in diverting this teacher from the material she had prepared. Since she
treated every enquiry with earnest seriousness, and apparently never
recognized flippant or mocking intentions, it was in fact very easy to
alter the direction of her lessons.

My reasons for choosing to study Latin with this teacher had to do
with her description of what the subject would entail. She spoke of
Aeneas' mysterious journey, of the love poems of Catullus, of the
dangerous political world which Cicero wrote about. It sounded like
another version of English, which for me had been by far the most

engrossing part of my school curriculum. And Latin, as taught by this teacher, did prove very much as I had anticipated. The texts we worked through were every bit as interesting, as moving, as human, as she had described them. My own progress in the subject also went well. Apparently impossible grammar seemed eventually, under this teacher's tuition, to become understandable. I found myself acquiring a large vocabulary, and even sometimes a sense of the rhythms of the language.

Yet, for all their interest and enjoyment, these Latin lessons involved complicated feelings. I found my own position ambiguous. Among my friends I had for a long time played my part in maintaining and elaborating an unkind mockery of this particular teacher. Now, in my Latin lessons, I experienced unmistakable affection from her. I was caught up in her own wide learning and real love for the subject she was teaching. I found gradually that I could not enter into the public currency of jokes against her; scripture lessons became increasingly painful occasions for me. My private learning, which made me 'special', was both treasured and embarrassing. It involved an experience of the teacher which could not be shared with friends who knew her very differently. The relationship set me apart, cut me off from my social group in this area of our school lives.

What was this learning about? To say that I learned Latin does not seem adequately to encompass it. I did develop an understanding of certain classical Latin texts. But this understanding was framed by the outlook of one particular teacher, coloured by her feelings, her unique sense of the meaning and vitality of the writings. In coming to appreciate Virgil's poetry, I came to approach it from a particular angle, to take the direction towards it which my teacher somehow conveyed. By doing so, I necessarily changed my position towards the teacher herself, and this act subtly but irrevocably altered my position towards my friends. My learning – for all its interest and enjoyment, its opening of new horizons – was personally costly. It entailed complicated and painful feelings to do with loyalty and betrayal, solidarity and loneliness.

How, most basically, do we see education? A certain story, containing the essence of many age-old myths and fairy tales, is widely if implicitly shared. After an arduous search, a mysterious and sometimes dangerous journey, the brave and tenacious adventurer at last achieves his or her reward – gaining the keys of the kingdom. The world with all its treasures – of knowledge, understanding, the whole cultural heritage – lies open for the taking. This is a story which sets the hardships, the confusion, the struggle of the learning endeavour against the richness of its prize. In its happy-ever-after ending, the learner who has stayed the whole long course, passed through each successive educational trial, triumphantly attains the ultimate goal – access to a world of understanding. It is in these terms that we usually see things. But what if we took another metaphor? Suppose we looked at the process of education as a version of the story of Adam and Eve.

For Kelly himself, the biblical parable of the Garden of Eden is the basic story of humanity. In an essay which he calls 'Sin and psychotherapy' he explores something of its meaning, by reflecting on the situation of a middle-aged client who has tried all his life to return to the Eden he knew in early childhood. Like Adam, like all of us, this man cannot go back there. By eating the forbidden fruit, Adam and Eve have come to a knowledge of good and evil. And this is fateful knowledge. Through seeing moral possibilities where none existed before, we lose our simple delight in the way things are. The world cannot be accepted without question ever again; our knowledge of what might be makes us restless, keeps us searching. We can no longer take everything for granted. We now possess, for better or worse, 'the awful responsibility for distinguishing good from evil'. There is no going back to the innocence we shared with animals and birds, to the paradise of our pre-moral world.

In the story we usually tell of education, the quest ends when learners take their hard-earned reward and, following their arduous endeavours, come at last into their own. But if our story is of paradise lost, this is only the beginning. Knowledge has consequences. The story of Adam and Eve does not end with their eating of the apple – or even with the expulsion from paradise which followed it. Knowing what they now know, Adam and Eve cannot but live out the moral possibilities they grasp:

> With knowledge come responsibilities, and with responsibilities come trouble. Adam and Eve, in this remarkably insightful story, sought the knowledge of good and evil, and that is precisely what they got, for they lived to see one of their sons grow to be a good man, and the other his murderer.
>
> (*Maher, 1969, pp. 166–7*)

In such a view, knowledge is not the end of the story, but rather the beginning of a new, qualitatively different chapter. It is a chapter involving the transformation of the protagonist. The questing knight of the traditional tale does not himself change when at last his mission is accomplished. But Adam and Eve are irrevocably altered by the knowledge they acquire. Adam starts to experience a new, disturbing self-consciousness. Once happily unaware of himself as a separate being, he now finds he is alone and embarrassingly exposed; he sees with shame that he must cover his nakedness. In coming to know the world differently, we ourselves are changed.

We think of knowledge, insight, understanding, as worthwhile in altogether simple ways. For learners struggling with their task, the treasures to be gained are of pure gold. Skies are cloudless in the kingdom of understanding. Yet, like Adam, we may find that we must buy our knowledge dearly. What we know may make us lonely in our social worlds. It may impose responsibilities we would far rather not possess. It is not only martyrs who, like Galileo, may have to suffer for what they come to know. The small girl whose elder brother insists on proving to her that Father Christmas is not real must give up a specially delightful part of her early childhood. Christmas is now for ever changed; the magic cannot be recaptured. To those British people for whom the Second World War was the noble struggle of a brave little island under its heroic leader, later revelations of the Dresden bombing, the betrayal of the Cossacks, were wholly repugnant, representing knowledge to be acquired with the greatest reluctance.

In Kelly's philosophy, our personal construct systems define the understanding we each live by. This means that learning is never the acquisition of a single, isolated bit of knowledge. Our ways of seeing things are inextricably intertwined. To alter one assumption means that others, too, are brought into question. Understanding has implications; a change in one idea entails possibilities of having to rethink others. And this is as true of school knowledge as of informal understanding. If art is really a matter of colour, where does this leave all those careful drawings you do at home, to the pleasure and admiration of your parents? Does this exciting new approach to mathematics render invalid all your earlier understanding of computation? Or, now that you begin to see how human affairs have always been affected by race, gender and social class, must the whole of history be rethought?

Some of the implications of learning involve risks that extend into the future. If as a girl you pursue your present fascination with molecular theory, where will it take you? Doing a physics option will put you among boys, and lead in directions very unlike those many of your friends are taking. If you follow up interesting English studies, with consequences for the way you speak, you may find that you have become alienated from your own background. Going on with your guitar lessons might entail discovering, in the end, that you cannot make it to the top.

As Adam found, to live by understanding rather than obedience means entering the difficult realm of existential choice. We have to give up the security of ignorance – the known boundaries to thinking and experience, the safety of shared ideas, the comfort of taking things for granted. Nor is it only individual 'learners' whose security is threatened by new ways of knowing. Societies are grounded in shared assumptions about human reality. To call any of those basic assumptions into question is to risk moving beyond the pale – into martyrdom, or madness. For most of us such possibilities are remote. But even much more limited extensions of understanding inevitably entail a questioning of conventional ideas, a refusal to be bound by traditional, established assumptions. As such, they pose their own challenge to the *status quo*.

In Kelly's philosophy, we construct and reconstruct what we know about ourselves and our world. But this does not mean that each of us must reinvent the wheel. Knowledge does not exist merely in our heads; it is also out there, enshrined in laws, in cultural artefacts, in established practices. Though understanding arises only out of the interrogations that, as human beings, we put to our world, once acquired it takes on an independent existence, an authority. Cumulatively, it provides the whole frame of reference within which as individuals we construct the meaning of our experience.

No one can step outside culture, or develop terms that entirely bypass its general frame of reference. Yet cultural understandings differ across space and time. What we know, we know as members of a culture which has its own distinctive interpretations of reality. But these interpretations can never be final, only provisional. They remain open, potentially, to reconstruction. In every epoch, through the struggles of groups and individuals, new themes, new issues become salient, with resulting change to social practices.

As Kelly insists, construct systems are personal. But this does not make them solipsistic. Though each of us inhabits a unique experiential world, meanings, if they are to be viable, must be built together with others. The human enterprise depends on a sharing of social reality. The sense which we make of our lives must also make some sense to others.

Human realities, first and foremost, are social realities. Personal meanings have their essential currency in relations between people, rather than within some wholly private world. Right from the beginning of life interpretations – the meanings to be accorded to things – are offered and exchanged between infants and their caregivers. As babies grow into childhood, the conversational confirmations, challenges, comparisons, interrogations of personal meaning grow at an exponential rate. A widening social experience brings awareness of competing realities, of alternative constructions. Somehow these must be met and negotiated. A personal system of meaning has to be forged which is viable, liveable, yet which remains open rather than closed.

Education in this psychology is the systematic interface between personal construct networks of meaning. This view puts as much emphasis on teachers' meanings as on those of learners. In most educational psychology, the knowledge which teachers bring is seen as essentially standard. This presupposes that knowledge itself is absolute. If you believe that history, science and mathematics embody their own ultimate truths about the world, then it is possible to see teachers of these subjects as all representing the same expertise.

But if knowledge is provisional, this view becomes untenable. Learning is not a matter of acquiring 'nuggets of truth', a treasure-house of human certainties. In learning, so far from achieving final answers, we find instead new questions, the need to try things further. Knowledge is ultimately governed by constructive alternativism; everything can always be reconstrued. Reality is not to be pinned down forever in a standardized curriculum. The understanding which teachers offer is necessarily provisional – for the time being only. And for all that school knowledge has high social consensus and is grounded in the whole cultural heritage, it is also indelibly personal. It takes its significance from within the construct system of any particular teacher. Since each person inhabits a distinctive world of meaning, the curriculum of education is constructed afresh, and individually, by every teacher who offers it.

Our personal construct systems carry what, in the broadest possible sense, each of us knows. It is these systems which allow us to 'read' our lives psychologically. They locate us, moment to moment, within events. They govern the stances we take up. They represent our possibilities of action, the choices we can make. They embody the dimensions of meaning which give form to our experience, the kinds of interpretation which we place on it. Since none of us can know anything of the world except through the meanings we have available to us, the dimensions we have constructed – our personal constructs – are crucially important. Of course these dimensions are not isolated and separate. Our experience of the world is complex, all of a piece, not a succession of different and unrelated categorizations. Constructs are interwoven within a whole system of meaning.

It is this interrelationship that produces the richness of implication, the complexity, the depth of any human perception. Meeting a new class, the experienced teacher instantly gets the feeling of a tricky group. The perception carries with it a whole network of interpretations – of past experience, future expectations, possible strategies and potential outcomes. These constructions define the teacher's position towards the group: assumptions about them, the kinds of engagement possible. They are likely to be available to the teacher, not as explicit verbal labels, but rather as an implicit set of inner guidelines towards the situation, felt and sensed rather than put inwardly into words. Our construct systems encompass far more than we could possibly say; and the more fundamental the knowledge, the less accessible it is to explicit verbalization.

Given in his formal writing to highly polysyllabic expression, Kelly defined his approach to learning as constructive alternativism, as against what he called accumulative fragmentalism. These somewhat daunting terms convey what is fundamentally distinctive in this philosophy of education.

Constructive alternativism proclaims the idea that what we know is essentially a construction. This is not to say that there is not a real world there at all, but that we can know it only though the interpretations we come to place upon it. We may think that we see directly, straightforwardly, that we know reality as it is. It may seem that nothing interposes itself between ourselves and the simple facts. But this is an illusion. As Kelly puts it, 'Events do not come bearing labels on their backs'. It is we who give meaning to things, who place our constructions on the world we inhabit – and these constructions are inseparable from our own human intentions and purposes, our agency and practices.

In this approach understanding is essentially constructive, a meaning put upon some aspect of our lives. The world we live in, psychologically, is a world constructed out of the whole history of human engagement within it. And therein lies the significance of Kelly's second term. Meanings are not to be pinned down for ever; there is always the possibility of an alternative construction. What differs above all between diverse societies is their way of seeing the world, their way of valuing and of living human life. The story of culture is the story of the shifts and changes over time in the meanings given to the peopled world. And between individuals, variations in personal experience and social positioning mean that one person sees life in terms that may be very different from those of another.

Human meanings in this philosophy are not unchanging, not for ever fixed. For education, this carries profoundly important implications. 'Whatever exists can be reconstrued', insists Kelly (1955, p. 26). It is because in any situation different constructions are always possible – there are always other, possibly more fruitful ways of looking at things – that personal construct psychology offers such a strong endorsement of educational potentiality. Though, as Adam found, abandoning previous convictions may be difficult and costly, it is only by venturing to try out a different kind of understanding that life itself may become transformed.

The vision of learning as transformative is intrinsic to constructive alternativism. The contrasting approach, accumulative fragmentalism, carries no such perspective. Accumulative fragmentalism might in fact very well serve to underpin the market model of education. The learning process, in this view, consists of the steady accumulation of more and more bits of unrelated knowledge; nuggets of truth, as Kelly calls them. Like the collection of items in the shopping trolley, understandings are separate from each other, without any intricate network of mutual linkages. They simply make up a growing pile. To a Kellyan, such a pile would look highly precarious. The next purchase might bring the whole edifice crashing down. But for an accumulative fragmentalist, the addition of a box of tissues, a packet of washing powder, does no more than bring one more item to sit at the top, leaving the other merchandise quite unaffected.

In personal construct psychology, understandings are deeply and complexly interrelated. This means that personally significant learning is never entirely risk-free. The way we see things is not merely a reflection, a gloss put on firmly established living practices. It is actually through our understandings that we constitute our ways of being in the world. Out of our constructs we construct our very lives.

New ways of looking at the world mean, in the end, altered ways of living. Different understandings are therefore always potentially threatening. And where new knowledge seems to challenge the fundamental basis of our identity, our established ways of doing things, it is likely of necessity to be resisted. Without some firm subjective anchor, some sense of personal grounding, no one can afford to launch themselves out into uncharted waters.

For many people, learning is a simple matter of experience. Expose someone to a new situation, such a person might say, and they will pick up what is going on. Noting what is happening and how things are, just putting two and two together; we do it all the time, without even realizing that we are learning. And yet, as Kelly remarks, the 20 years' experience of which someone continually boasts may be no more than one year repeated 20 times. Although, as human beings, we all possess a vast capacity for learning, it is also remarkable how much we do not learn.

Our human status is, as Kelly argues, a delicately balanced one. Venture too far beyond commonly accepted realities, or out of socially established identity, and we put at risk a viable way of living. But settling comfortably, safely and for ever into what counts as common sense carries its own dangers too. For even the most copper-bottomed certainties may one day fall apart. As Kelly writes, we may then experience

> the failure of those truths that have served to make so many days turn out as expected. We believe them because how else is one to know what is really so, or how else to bridge the chasm between past and future over which we always find ourselves suspended, and how else to find continuity and thus live these 'truths'. They may be little tick-tick-tick-tick truths that keep repeating themselves in the corner – or they can be big round shining truths, brittle as all perfect things must be – that roll along majestically until they crash against the day that was not meant for them, and leave you with nothing, but their fragments – a litter of words – leave you shattered too.
> (*Kelly, 1978, p. 227*)

Human learning carries both large dangers and large opportunities. And it is at the borders of these that the world of teaching stands. Much classroom learning material – an agenda imposed to some degree on teachers and pupils alike – may seem so peripheral as to be entirely devoid of personal risk. Yet, as many teachers are all too well aware, the connotations of a broadly monocultural curriculum, in which sexism and classism are frequently built in, may give it a personal meaning for many pupils which is nothing if not threatening.

To the extent that it validates the norms and values, the ways of living of certain social groupings, schooling can implicitly demean or exclude those of others. In the Christianity purveyed in school assemblies or religious education, for instance, Jews may be portrayed as murderers of Jesus Christ. Some classroom materials define Black people as coming from, and therefore belonging, 'somewhere else'. When formal learning fails to take, this may not only be because it is so boring. Resistance may also arise because of the insult implicitly offered to personal and social identity.

Teaching calls for sensitivity and imagination; for an awareness of pupils' personal construct systems, the richly varied realities which children bring to classroom learning. In conveying the meaning of the official school curriculum, teachers have to attend to, and appreciate, a diverse range of existing understandings. If new, potentially enlarging understandings are to be ventured, they must make at least some initial sense to learners; they must have some meaning within current constructions. And this meaning has to be one which respects, rather than threatens, personally fundamental assumptions – those that underpin pupils' norms, values and allegiances, their very sense of themselves and those they love. All this means that fruitful classroom negotiations of meaning – between formal and personal knowledge systems – necessarily involve tact and delicacy.

Personal construct psychology does not oversimplify the complexity, the sheer difficulty, of the whole learning enterprise. It does not insult teachers by portraying their work in facile, superficial terms. But as an educational approach, it invests the very highest value in learning, in the refusal to settle for established wisdom, for taken-for-granted realities, in the insistence on continually daring to question what is known: 'The living history of man is the story of the questions he has enacted, rather than the conclusions he has anchored in science or dogma. ... In reaching terminal conclusions, man commits the ultimate suicide of his race' (Maher, 1966, pp. 12–13).

Chapter 3

Teachers and Teaching

> By sharing their encounters with events – including the events pro-
> duced by their own behaviour – [people] do develop a fair understand-
> ing, each of what the other is talking about. ... Children and men,
> therefore, cease to be altogether alone when they try to see events
> through the spectacles others use, even while reserving the privilege of
> using their own.
> (*Maher, 1969, p. 28*)

Ask anyone about their most significant experiences in learning,
and they will almost certainly start talking about the people who
taught them. That awkward, memorable young man, whose own
ardent passion for mathematics created from a dry-as-dust subject a
distinctive, fascinating world. The woman English teacher, with her
undaunted faith in you, who finally enabled you to break through
your writing block. The brilliant and sarcastic person who exposed
your early attempts at painting to public ridicule, and left you perma-
nently and hopelessly convinced of your own artistic ineptitude.

For very many people, teachers seem to have been the key that
opened – or locked – the door to personally meaningful kinds of
learning. And this is not only a retrospective feeling. In children's talk
of daily classroom experience, the figures of their teachers loom large.
For those at school teachers are not at all much of a muchness, but
highly differentiated. This is the case for primary as well as secondary
age, for boys as for girls, for pupils alienated from school work, just as
for highly motivated pupils.

All children, in their experience of classroom learning, seem to have
a keen sense of their teachers as very different and distinctive kinds of

people. This sense of difference is typically quite complex, and goes a long way beyond merely feeling that some teachers are good and others bad. In discussing any teacher, children convey something of a particular personal world, a world with its own atmosphere, its own possibilities. It is a world where certain things can happen, where certain expectations operate. And in this world you experience particular kinds of feeling, even become a particular kind of person.

Accounts of teaching typically portray it in terms of a generalized character, often as competences unrelated to particular curriculum content. But to teachers themselves, what they teach is surely not a matter of indifference. Explaining this choice of profession, the young beginning teacher refers to his enthusiasm for his subject, a sense that children, too, could find it interesting, exciting. As the primary teacher discusses tomorrow's plans, it is the value, the significance of the work the teacher wants the children to do, that she emphasizes. And looking back over his teaching career, its triumphs and its disappointments, the retiring head of English dwells on his changing curriculum. How reluctant he had been to abandon the old way, the single standard form of grammar and pronunciation, to be mastered by every pupil! You knew what you were doing, what you were aiming for; you could tell young people when they had got things right. But that other way, for all you resisted it at the time, proved in the end so much better, with its recognition of linguistic diversity, giving every pupil a place in the classroom. And now the wheel has turned full circle, and it is back to the bad old ways, with all their proven limitations.

For an approach that takes human subjectivity seriously, any understanding of teachers is unviable if it makes no reference to the curriculum they teach. A Kellyan view, with its emphasis on the personal construction of meaning, must have a good deal to say about the content which teachers themselves see as so important. Far from describing a teacher in terms distinct from his or her curriculum, in this perspective you are yourself, in some sense, what you teach.

What would it mean to take this approach, to see the content of teaching as intrinsically personal to each particular teacher? Teaching would be viewed, not as the passing on of a parcel of objective knowledge, but as the attempt to share with others what you yourself find personally meaningful. It is the teacher's own sense of the richness of history, the wonder of the physical world, that makes the lesson exciting; where pupils catch fire, it is the teacher's fire they catch. And this is a uniquely personal fire. One teacher's Spanish is not the Spanish of her colleague; though the syllabus may be the same, the lessons are not. What gives importance, value, vitality to one person's material is hers alone; and it is this – or its absence – which is the real substance of her teaching.

For as everyone knows, not all teaching is exciting, and lessons may be very boring, for teachers as well as children. If we think of the curriculum as personal, it does not really seem very surprising that teachers are often uncomfortable with the content of their teaching. This is not just a matter of gradually losing a sense of the liveliness of the subject over years and years of daily classroom grind. Since the freedom of teachers is increasingly constrained, it is not uncommon to to find someone obliged to put over a curriculum which she does not like, cannot respect, and does not personally value.

For many people who teach in schools, the resources and texts which constitute much of the curriculum impose unacceptable limits and directions on what may be taught. How is it possible, when you are all too aware of colonial exploitation and its dire consequences for many of those in your multicultural classroom, to teach from books which glorify British explorers, British conquests? Even in the re-worked history curriculum the beneficence bestowed by colonialism goes generally unquestioned. There are also other kinds of alienation for those who teach. A young teacher of biology, keenly aware of animal rights, can only feel a constant inner protest if working in an old-fashioned department which still routinely dissects animal corpses. For a home economics teacher strongly concerned to engage boys in her curriculum, the timetable which forces a choice between this subject and technology must impose a meaning on her classroom work which runs entirely counter to the teacher's own values.

If teaching means offering others your personal sense of the curriculum, then feelings of alienation from what you teach have to be taken seriously. What such feelings may mean emerges from a piece of research carried out a decade ago by two psychologists working in London, Rosie Walden and Valerie Walkerdine (1985). These researchers were interested in exploring how it is that girls, who start off as good as or better than boys in mathematics gradually fall behind in the subject, generally ending up mathematically incompetent.

There has of course long been a concern with this question, which has been viewed as one aspect of the gender stereotyping of school knowledge. Mathematics and science are characteristically seen as objective, high-level, high-status, and quintessentially male subjects. Languages and the arts, in contrast, are seen as softer, less rigourous subjects – for girls rather than for boys. As another consequence of the stereotyping process, men typically end up teaching the 'male' subjects, and women the 'female' ones. So one solution has been to reverse this logic and to employ, for instance, women mathematics teachers.

It was this situation which Walden and Walkerdine examined. They studied the position of women mathematics teachers at primary and secondary levels, watching them teach and talking to them and to their pupils about their classroom work. What emerged showed how complicated it was for a woman to teach mathematics. In part this is because the curriculum of school mathematics had, at that period, its own kind of gender-related content. In the early stages of primary mathematics, problems were located in the domestic world – the traditional sphere of girls and women. But gradually this changed, so that by secondary age the content had become stereotypically male – the world of mechanics and engineering. What would this have meant for a woman teaching the subject?

At early stages of the subject, the primary woman teacher, in her daily classroom work, is 'at home'. The problems she talks about with her pupils are those of her own traditional domain. As Walden and Walkerdine remark: 'In early Mathematics, domestic tasks (weighing, measuring, shopping) are used as a matter of course. This allows stereotypically feminine activities to be used as the site for the teaching of Mathematics' (Walden and Walkerdine, 1985, p. 6).

These activities are part of the whole world with which the teacher, as a woman, is likely to be very familiar. They relate to spheres which the boys and girls in her class expect her to know about, to be expert in. But later in the secondary classroom, things have become different. The woman mathematics teacher is now talking about areas of experience with which she is likely to be rather unfamiliar, to feel something of a stranger. And even if this is not so, for the pupils in her class these areas do not belong to her. Nor do they, by this stage, belong to the girls in the class; they are part of the whole domain that has been claimed by the boys.

Recent years have seen a growing awareness of the ways in which the school curriculum can carry implicit messages about gender.

Concern has centred in particular on the content of computer programs, as adding their own contribution to girls' sense of exclusion from the sphere of computer technology. But altering curriculum materials to make them more girl-friendly is tackling only one aspect of a complex situation. As Walden and Walkerdine found, being female in the world of school also has implications to do with power and status.

The ambiguity of the position held by the women studied in this research was characteristic, not just of their relations with the content of what they taught, but also of their place in the school's authority structure. Just as the highest status is typically accorded to curriculum areas defined as male, so those holding positions of relative power, at least at secondary level, tend to be men. This is as true of ancillary as it is of teaching staff. It is not only that head teachers tend to be male. The more powerful job of caretaker is typically held by a man, as against the humbler post of cleaner, who is almost invariably a woman. For a woman, teaching mathematics puts her in an anomalous position. The authority bestowed by the high status of her subject is at the same time implicitly undermined by her own gender.

From the observations which these researchers made, all this had a profound effect on how these women taught. In contrast with their general ease and confidence in primary classrooms, women mathematics teachers within the secondary sector were typically uneasy, diffident, uncertain of their role. This sense of insecurity was most evident in their dealings with boys, towards whom they were often deferential, sometimes even apologetic. Of course something of these teachers' discomfort was communicated to their pupils, thereby reinforcing the very message which teaching appointments like these were meant to counter.

If the curriculum to be taught were really separate from the particular teacher who offers it, then setting up women to teach mathematics would solve, once and for all, the problem of its stereotyping by gender. The fact that this solution turns out to be far from simple, and may sometimes actually make things worse, must mean that what people teach is inseparable from who they are. Personal construct psychology does not make the traditional separation between the knower and the known. The curriculum of teaching cannot be an independent entity; teachers and their subjects are intimately interlinked.

Conventionally, we talk as though expertise in a subject were a question of mastering a standard body of material: the sequence of recorded historical events, or the interrelated principles of physics. We assume that, apart from slight differences in emphasis, two experts possess essentially the same knowledge, have identical, insiders' views. Yet this assumption cannot be fitted with the idea that knowledge is essentially a construction.

In this perspective, expertise takes on a very different character to the one we usually give it. If people construct what they know through their personal engagements in the social world, then we must necessarily see each person's body of knowledge as in some sense unique. Expertise then becomes, not the possession of a standard package of material acquired from others at second hand, but an intricate personal landscape through which to move at will from one interesting vista to another.

Of course our understanding of the world, of our own human realities, exists at different levels. What we most deeply know – what we feel in our bones to be true – represents a different order of knowledge from, say, the technicalities of the Dutch grammar we are now teaching ourselves. And it is perhaps the relation between these two levels of understanding that is, above all, the concern of Kellyan psychology.

How explicit knowledge actually relates to deeper levels of knowing is profoundly important. It is possible, for instance, to have quite an elaborate system of knowledge about some area which has only slight personal significance. Because an old banger is all you can afford, you have had of necessity to learn a lot about motor mechanics. But this knowledge is purely instrumental. You can talk as well as anyone about big ends and blowing gaskets, but you really find the whole topic of cars extremely boring. It cannot compare with the personal investment, the emotional depth, of your interest in music. From this point of view, it is the degree to which an area of understanding touches the deepest, most personal roots of what we know, that represents our real commitment to it.

The interrelation of different kinds of knowledge may be quite complicated. For the women mathematics teachers whom Walden and Walkerdine studied, their experience could be defined as involving contradictions in what they knew. The explicit understanding they expressed as mathematics teachers could not sit easily with the deep understandings they possessed as women. What we know is, in the end, knowledge of ourselves. And these women, within their particular society, were struggling with two apparently incompatible kinds of knowledge. In a sense they lacked integrity: the harmony between our conscious, verbalized knowledge, and what in our bones we really know to be true.

If we see teaching like this, we have to take another perspective to the usual one on differences between teachers. Traditionally, teachers have been seen as good or bad, competent or incompetent, more or less effective. That implies an essential commonality of aim, of material; it views teachers as all trying to do the same thing, and doing it more or less well. But if knowledge is essentially a construction, a construction which ramifies into what is deeply personal, into the inarticulate as well as the explicit, then in teaching, every teacher is doing something unique.

When we teach, in a sense we teach ourselves. As teachers, we are not merely the gateway to knowledge. We ourselves represent, embody our curriculum. And in our teaching, we convey not just our explicit knowledge, but also our position towards it – the personal ramifications and implications which it has for us. This means that teaching is not exactly a matter of doing some standard thing well or badly. The question is rather, *what* is being taught? The boredom, the bad faith, the inner doubts about the material; all this comes over just as clearly as the sense of richness, excitement, possibility which it may invoke. Teachers may often teach their own positive stance towards the curriculum they offer. But sometimes, standing estranged from what they teach, they cannot but convey unclear, complicated messages – secret reservations, personal alienation, an inner discomfort with the content they ostensibly put over.

In Kellyan perspective, teaching seems to be quite a personal affair. So also does it in the philosophy of Carl Rogers (1983), whose ideas, inspiring for many educationists, have sometimes been compared with those of Kelly. Like Kelly, Rogers sees learning not as an alien task to be imposed on learners, but as something intrinsic to human character – unless, that is, the impulse has been suppressed through the failure to find unconditional acceptance.

Neither Kelly nor Rogers sees teaching as a matter of instruction. In a Rogerian philosophy, it represents the facilitation of innate strivings towards personal development. For the teacher, this entails providing a safe, affirming context. Blocks in learning arise through fear: fear that following personal directions might jeopardize the approval of important others. Only by sharing secret and perhaps incoherent ideas and feelings with another person, someone caring and sensitive, someone who does not pass judgement, may it be possible to dissolve such blocks, to regain the confidence for further human development.

In the two approaches there are also other parallels. Both men were psychotherapists; both see an essential similarity between therapeutic and educational endeavours. For Rogers, good outcomes depend on personal qualities in the therapist/teacher. The ideal person has the capacity for empathy with others; is able to sense, to read, another's deepest feelings. Personal warmth is also needed; the ability to sustain caring and affection despite occasional moments of irritation. And most importantly, the teacher must be an honest, truthful person, not someone who is apt to put on a false front from time to time. If teachers pretend to feel what they do not feel, to disguise their own responses, they cannot hope to inspire learners to trust the inner feelings which guide and underpin the deepest learning.

Warmth, sincerity, non-possessiveness: these are attributes of individual personality. Such personalized qualities make no reference to the social and cultural constitution of human beings. And it is here that a Kellyan understanding of education parts company with a Rogerian one. In personal construct psychology, the practice of teaching, the persons of teachers and learners, cannot be divorced from their social contexts and positions, from the cultural constraints and possibilities within which their personal realities have developed.

In Rogerian terminology, teachers are facilitators. This term, abstract and generalized as it is, conjures up a vague, blurred silhouette, not quite a person; someone mysteriously devoid of age and gender, race and class, someone with no particular social or professional identity. Yet every teacher is surely and indelibly marked by social and by cultural characteristics. And it is as very particular social presences that children in classrooms encounter their teachers.

Social class is one such parameter. As the newly appointed teacher walks in, everything about her – how she dresses, stands, speaks – proclaims middle class status. For the working class young people who are to be her pupils, this status cannot but have initially distancing implications. As a major dimension of social differentiation, it will inevitably govern how, at least to begin with, they read the teacher and the curriculum she offers them; the kind of stance they take towards her. For children as for adults, a different social class means other values, alien concerns, unfamiliar personal worlds.

Pupils do not as a rule construe their teachers in such explicitly sociological terms. Social and cultural characteristics are more likely to be experienced as an integral part of a global personal impression. Here is the new teacher; your previous teacher has left to have a baby. For you, a 6-year-old girl in the class, he is obviously, disturbingly different. The lady teacher was small and young and pretty, she was kind, and spoke in a quiet voice. This new teacher is quite old, and very tall and big. He has a loud voice, especially when he laughs. Before, you were getting on very well with your reading, and your mother was pleased with the books you took home. But now there isn't much reading or writing, because you are always doing things in a big group. Your previous teacher always used to come up to the children, but this one calls out to you in front of the whole class. Everyone hears what you say, and often the teacher makes a joke about it, and they all roar with laughter.

This same teacher, so intimidating to one small girl in the class, may be quite differently construed by the boy sitting next to her. For this pupil the teacher's encouragement of group activity, his tolerance of high levels of noise and movement in the room, his constant jokes and laughter, may come as a welcome relief. The teacher's large, masculine physical presence seems comfortable, reassuring, enlivening. School, previously a place of difficulty and boredom, is now good fun, something to look forward to. Yet even for this pupil, mixed with his sense of exhilaration may be other less positive feelings. School, after all, is supposed to mean quiet and serious work; this teacher's ways produce, at times, a sense of doubt, almost of guilt.

In this imaginary classroom, it is not only the children who engage in this kind of construing. In taking on his group, the teacher must make his own sense of the particular social identities within it – including the little girl who seems so shy and ill at ease, who responds so little, so mistrustfully to his suggestions and his jokes. If things are not to crystallize for ever in this initial fixture of difficult relations, this teacher must find some way of meeting his pupil's constructions. Genuinely personal encounters, personal dialogue, can proceed only out of sociality.

Our society is not, of course, homogeneous and monocultural. And for a teacher to grasp something of the personal reality experienced by a pupil from a different cultural group is not easy. It demands an imaginative understanding of young people as building their unique lives from the particular socio-cultural materials available to them – and in the process partly transforming the meanings of those materials. It means seeing features that are shared by members of that cultural group, but also seeing beyond them; being aware of commonalities, but not being dominated by these as simple stereotypes.

This kind of educational effort is a parallel with the task which, as Kelly describes it, faces a psychotherapist working with a client from a different cultural tradition. This is his account of a gentile psychotherapist newly encountering Jewish clients:

> The gentile therapist who comes in contact with a series of Jewish clients for the first time may be baffled by the similarities he sees in contrast with his other clients. If he is to understand them as persons rather than to stereotype them, he must neither ignore the cultural expectations under which they have validated their constructs – expectations of both Jewish and gentile groups – nor make the mistake of focussing on the group constructs to the exclusion of the personal constructs of each group. If he stops with group constructs he does an injustice to his clients. If he sees group constructs as the elements upon which his clients have had to form personal constructs about themselves and their companions, he may come to understand the obstacles and aspirations which play such an important part in their personal readjustment.
> (*Kelly, 1955, pp. 181–2*)

These concerns relate, in Kellyan terminology, to questions of commonality and, especially, sociality. Commonality, as the establishing of shared interest, agreed perspectives and meanings held in common, is of course the explicit goal of the whole educational undertaking. But it is the operation of sociality which is critical to its attainment. Sociality means 'a broad and sensitive attention to how another construes his world'. It represents the willingness and capacity to step into another person's shoes; to begin to see the world as that person sees it, to adopt, for the moment, the terms and dimensions of meaning through which that person makes sense of things. In this, a teacher's way of working may again resemble that of a psychotherapist. For both, as Kelly suggests, this is partly a question of language: 'The therapist should try to employ the client's vocabulary ... he should give words the meanings that the client gives them, rather than the meanings the dictionary gives them, or the personal and professional meanings he has himself customarily given them' (Kelly, 1955, p. 587).

What this can entail in practice is illustrated in an account offered by Douglas Barnes (1986), a life-long student of language across the curriculum. As he argues, school learning means making connections between the action knowledge of day-to-day experience and the specialized knowledge of the classroom. The language which teachers themselves use can act to make these connections closer. In a book written together with James Britton and Mike Torbe, Barnes uses the example of a physics teacher. Rather than insisting that his pupils master the subject's technical vocabulary, this teacher offers them space to try out their own formulations of what is happening. To encourage this, he himself speaks in highly untechnical language:

> This is almost the same as that one ... a slightly different arrangement ... cut in half ... you see it? ... little tin can ... silver thing in the middle, ... silver thing with circles on it? ... that's that tin can ... tin can just like that one ... all right ... on a good day then what is going to happen to the shape of that? Is it going to go ... down? ... Do you know? ... See what happens to the pointer. Well that pointer is going to be connected....
> (*Barnes, 1986, p. 68*)

As Barnes relates, the pupils in this lesson were boys and girls of quite limited ability. Nevertheless, they became actively involved in this physics demonstration, attending closely and questioning the teacher about what they saw. This must, he suggests, have been related to the way their teacher talked. The importance of his language was not just that, though informal, it was exactly adjusted to the apparatus. More significantly, this linguistic mode carried a clear message for these pupils; that he was interested in their own understandings and their attempts to extend them. In attending to their struggle to understand as well as to his goals as a teacher of physics, this teacher was able to set up a real exchange of interpretations.

In Kelly's words, each of us lives by 'hearing the whisper of recurrent themes in the events which reverberate around us' (1955, p. 113). If teachers are to reach the young people who sit within their classrooms, they need to listen for widely varied yet distinctive themes. The teaching role is one demanding many kinds of understanding beyond those of the subject itself.

If, in their classroom work, teachers implicitly invite learners to adopt, at least provisionally, their own stance, this invitation is likely to seem more credible to some pupils than to others. In this, the teacher's own readier identification with certain young people must play a part. For all of us as adults, it is easy to enter into some children's lives – imaginable without effort because they seem comparable with our own childhoods. Envisaging what the curriculum could mean to such children – its potential meaningfulness, its richness for them – enables us to offer it with confidence. But for other young people, whose out-of-school lives are more mysterious, their identities less accessible to us, the message we offer may be less confident, less clear. Only by working to enlarge these limits of sociality is it possible to extend more widely the invitation which teaching essentially entails.

Good teachers, according to this view, are deeply thoughtful practitioners. Teaching involves both intellectual and feeling qualities, and a concern that can only be called moral. As a profession, it calls for an unusually high level of social and cultural consciousness. In Bruner's words, teachers need 'a willingness to construe knowledge and values from multiple perspectives, without loss of commitment to one's own values' (Bruner, 1990, p. 32). A role as rich, as complex, as difficult as this can certainly not be reduced to the narrow technical expertise – the subject knowledge and practical classroom skills – by which much present-day educational policy defines it.

The major site of ideological struggle in the construction of teachers and teaching, as John Furlong (1992) argues, is that of initial teacher education. Here, as he suggests, the government's operating principles have paralleled those that guided its attempts to engineer the National Curriculum. Just as the more critical, the more reflective areas of school learning were the target of early political interference in the curriculum, so the major disciplines of thought – philosophy, psychology, sociology – have, wherever possible, been excluded from initial teacher training. Redefined as the acquisition of craft knowledge, the whole process of professional development has been almost reduced to 'sitting by Nelly'. Of course in removing teacher training from institutes of higher education, the government intends to eliminate the influence of critical ideas.

At its most extreme, the wish to reduce the professional meaning of teaching – to abolish, once and for all, the reflective practitioner – was expressed in a recent published comment by the Conservative peer, Lord Skidelsky. This was the opinion he offered the House of Lords in their debate of the Education Bill:

I have had occasion to study professionally much of the research that has taken place, and I have also had experience in my own university. There is no theoretically-based good practice which defines professional teaching. I can think of few things more destructive of effective learning than a full understanding of educational theory. (*Skidelsky, 1994, p. 3*)

Bigotry as blatant as this is rare in public educational debate. But underlying such irrational comments must be a profound sense of threat, perhaps widely held in governing circles, from an autonomous teaching profession.

Chapter 4

Institutes of Schooling

Children are more and more caught up in the complex dependency matrix of global wants and fragmentary supplies that characterise modern adult life ... Playgrounds are supervised by specialists. Even joy has to come in pieces. Schools assume an increasing authority over the child's life, and then divide it up into departmentalized instruction – a further fragmentation of the child's sources of supply.
(*Maher, 1969, p. 192*)

I spent that first day picking holes in paper, then went home in a smouldering temper.
'What's the matter, Love? Didn't he like it at school then?'
'They never gave me the present.'
'Present? What present?'
'They said they'd give me a present.'
'Well, now, I'm sure they didn't.'
'They did. They said, "You're Laurie Lee, aren't you? Well, just you sit there for the present." I sat there all day, but I never got it. I ain't going back there again.'
(*Lee, 1965, p. 30*)

This sad little story is often quoted. Evidently, Laurie Lee's experience speaks to many people of their own. As they enter the door for their first day at school, probably most children look, and feel, ignorant and foolish. Yet by the age of five, any child is highly knowledgeable and has acquired a wide range of personal understanding. How is it that schools, set up with the best possible intentions, staffed by people who have children's interests at heart, so often fail to meet the child halfway, to engage with children on their own terms?

In Kellyan psychology we are defined by the understandings we have constructed, the world of meanings we deal in and inhabit. These understandings, these meanings, are not directly transmitted to us; we create them ourselves, through our engagements with the world. They are inseparable from our experience; the positions we have taken, the choices we have made, the undertakings we have launched. The knowledge of 5-year-old children cannot be divorced from their participation in life.

A decade ago, Barbara Tizard and Martin Hughes (1984) studied thirty 4-year-old girls, comparing the mornings they spent at nursery school with their afternoons at home. Since the focus of the study was talk, these little girls' conversations were all tape-recorded, through small microphones sewn into their clothes. The researchers were therefore able to make detailed comparisons between the children's talk with their nursery school teachers, and the conversations they had at home with their mothers. These comparisons yielded startling contrasts.

From their talk at home, these little girls emerge as 'persistently questioning, puzzling minds'; constantly demonstrating a lively intellectual curiosity. As they strive to understand a new word, grasp an unfamiliar idea, or fit new information into what they already know, the children are clearly searching, making strenuous efforts in an urgent quest for further knowledge. All this is very different from the way they appear in the context of nursery school. Here, they are subdued and passive towards adults, rather than talking spontaneously. Exchanges with teachers are typically short-lived and monosyllabic, consisting of minimal responses to questions. The tone of these exchanges is usually very low key and flat, in contrast with the liveliness of their conversations at home. Like Laurie Lee on his first day at school, these little girls appear intellectually far more limited than at home they show themselves to be.

On the face of it, this situation is paradoxical. Nursery schools are, after all, designed to be intellectually stimulating. Relative to most home settings in this study, they are extremely well furnished, and equipped with large- and small-scale play materials. Unlike mothers, nursery school teachers do not have to make room for their children amidst multiple domestic and family responsibilities. Though child numbers are much larger, teachers' attention and educational purpose are undivided.

As most nursery school teachers would readily acknowledge, the impetus to understanding is enquiry. We construct our world out of

the interrogations we make of it, the questions we put to it. In this
study, questions represent a major focus. These small girls constantly,
persistently, urgently question their mothers. Yet in the nursery
school setting, these same children apparently find nothing to ask of
their teachers; instead it is the teachers who ask questions. And
whereas, in their own questioning, the children launch long, often
complex conversational exchanges, the teachers' questioning typically fails to take off – falls flat. These questions do not lead to
learning. We can, it seems, develop understanding only through our
own enquiries. We cannot undertake new ventures within the terms of
someone else's initiative.

When people ask questions, they put particular aspects of their
experience at issue. Tizard and Hughes, in their analysis, looked at the
subject matter of the children's questions. As they chat with their
mothers – going about the ordinary business of domestic work,
feeding or changing the baby, or over a meal – these little girls are
characteristically preoccupied with some aspect of their everyday
lives. It is to family relationships, household affairs – the social world
they live in and know about – that their questions are addressed.

Located within the children's own daily lives, these questions
presuppose a shared social experience. And it just this shared experience which makes them, as enquiries, generally so fertile. What is
shared between questioned and questioner covers wide spans of time
and space. Little children and their mothers know many places, and
can make links across them. Both intimately share past as well as
present time; both have a lively anticipation of a shared future.

All this is very different from what is involved when nursery school
teachers put questions to their charges. In this study, such enquiries
typically centre on the child's use of play materials. Interpreting her
task in broadly Piagetian terms, the teacher seeks to develop intellectual understanding by interrogating the child about colour,
number, volume or causal relationships. The scope of such questions
is inevitably very limited. They are located in the here and now. It is
difficult for the teacher to make reference to the habitual activities,
interests or involvements of individual children. Her questions are
typically addressed, within a relatively impersonal context, to a generalized child, not to a particular participant within a personally
shared social order.

If children acquire, with eagerness and intensity, a rich array of
understanding about the social world of home, it is because in that

world they are themselves active agents. Even in the early years of life, children have their part to play in the family scene. It is as participants that they are involved, not as mere spectators of events.

As human beings of a particular age and gender, a particular place in the family, with particular personal characteristics, all children, no matter how young, have to create their own distinctive ways of taking part in the life of their household. They must, as members of that household, negotiate their own commitments, expectations and responsibilities. There is nothing trivial about all this. Small children do not just play at living. What they do, how they conduct themselves, is of real consequence to themselves and those around them. Their knowledge of their own social world is the outcome of their own serious engagement in it.

The idea that children learn through their own activity is of course not new. It represents the central building-block of the whole Piagetian edifice. As such it has exercised great influence on the organization of school learning, at least at primary level. Yet, as Margaret Donaldson (1978) has shown, it is not enough to provide children with opportunities for experimentation; we need to pay attention to context. In her terms, young children think in human, not in abstract terms. If we wish to engage them in thinking, we must do so through questions that are embedded in familiar contexts and activities, that make human rather than merely formal sense.

It seems likely that in many nursery schools and reception classes, teachers would define their teaching in just these terms. Typically much care is taken, in setting up young children's first encounters with the world of school, to make that world as *homely* as possible. Classroom furnishings are informal and cosy. The activities offered are essentially familiar rather than strange, with play being the major mode. The position of teachers towards their charges is not, apparently, far from a maternal role, involving support and care-giving at least as much as instruction. In all these ways, early school experience would be seen as an extension of home experience, rather than a departure from it.

On the evidence of the Tizard and Hughes study, this assumption of an essential comparability for young children between their two worlds is open to challenge. But it is also clearly the case that the continuities of school and home are much closer for some young children than for others. And here, social class plays a very significant part.

In a forceful analysis, Valerie Walkerdine and Helen Lucey (1989) acidly delineate the psychology underlying much early education: a psychology which, in equating mothering with teaching, takes mothers' domestic activities to represent the natural occasions for children's playful learning. This perspective, argue these writers, blithely ignores the daily pressures under which working class mothers manage their housework and their young children. Its image of a 'sensitive mother', so concerned with her child's learning that 'even the way she peels the potatoes becomes a site for proving her worth', (p. 77) is one to which middle class women, with their greater resources of time and money, may perhaps aspire. But working class life allows no such blurring between work and play. With a premium on time, domestic chores must be accomplished before a father gets home, or a mother goes off to work. In these circumstances children must learn not to interfere, to play by themselves, to be self-reliant. For a young working class child, play is likely to mean a far more delimited activity, and one which may carry no necessary adult involvement.

At every stage of education, learning will take only if it is consonant with the social realities and cultural modes of young people themselves. This recognition is made difficult by traditional ways of organizing schools. Implicitly these draw hard-and-fast lines between the social and the educational. And yet, as many teachers would insist, schools are themselves essentially social institutions.

A benign community of learning, open to its neighbourhood, contributing to local needs and welcoming every kind of local involvement. This, for many head teachers and their staffs, is the kind of school they have worked for. Such a vision has no place in current prescriptions. A good school is now constituted by its position in the hierarchy of league tables, its achievement of narrowly defined learning 'standards'. That, says current dogma, is what parents want. Yet research, where it has been done, tells a different story.

In a study of parental attitudes towards their children's primary schools, Martin Hughes and a group of his colleagues (Hughes *et al.*, 1993) found that almost universally it was the social, the human aspects of schooling which essentially counted. Personal accessibility, a happy and caring atmosphere, enthusiastic and sensitive teachers, learning methods which engaged their children actively; these factors, for the vast majority of mothers and fathers, greatly outweighed academic criteria in the way they evaluated schools.

To parents, their children do of course represent unique human beings, active agents with their own social interests and undertakings. And when schools manage to build bridges between their pupils' out-of-school lives and classroom work, this is something parents appreciate. Establishing such continuities has probably never been easy, especially at secondary level. But it has certainly been made far more difficult by the current narrowing of the educational agenda.

One example of this is the situation of personal and social education. This area of learning, with its potential for engaging the real life contexts and concerns of young people, has been marginalized within the school curriculum, and its scope much reduced.

What this can lead to is illustrated by the predicament of those who teach sex education in schools. As one teacher recently discovered, to offer honest answers about human sexual conduct to 9-year-olds is to court ministerial rebuke and an official public enquiry. Nor is this area of learning any less hedged about with restrictions at later age levels. Giving contraceptive advice to girls under 16 may, according to the guidance of the 1993 Education Act, constitute a criminal offence.

There are surely few people who would dispute the need to educate young people about human sexuality – its practices, regulation and potential consequences, its social, personal and emotional meanings. Puberty, especially in girls, now occurs much earlier than it did, and a significant number of 13-year-olds are already sexually active. Amidst the ever-present threat of AIDS, to withold vital information from concerned young people seems grossly irresponsible.

Unlike many kinds of school learning, sex education, if it was honestly taught, would actually be welcome to teenagers themselves. In a 1994 survey commissioned by the Health Education Authority, every one of the 503 13- to 15-year-olds questioned thought that all pupils should receive this teaching. And again unlike many educational inputs, such education stands to make a genuine impact on the lives of young people. The up-front approach of sex education in the Netherlands has been associated with a frequency of teenage pregnancies which is seven times lower than that of the UK.

If they are to engage the young in their own learning, schools must recognize and address pupils' living concerns. These are not, of course, the same for every pupil. But schools, as institutions, are typically impersonal places, and impose a standard role on all who enter through their gates. In our institutes of learning there is little room for acknowledging individual identity. For teachers, all too aware of the social diversity within their classrooms, conscious of the different homes and neighbourhoods, the diverse lives which pupils inhabit, the leeway for manoeuvre is increasingly hemmed in. Children living in poverty or in fear must be treated alike with those from safe and comfortable homes. The prescribed curriculum of schooling allows less and less differentiation between pupils who bring rich cultural capital to their classrooms, and pupils for whom the disjunction between home and school seems quite impossibly wide.

Of all those likely to suffer from the impersonality, the relentless standardization of schooling, children from ethnic and cultural minorities are probably the most vulnerable. Many hard-won resources with which to address their particular needs are now lost or under threat. The withdrawal, for instance, of central funding for special language support cannot but have seriously adverse effects on children from non-English-speaking homes.

But perhaps those who are now most at risk from a narrow and impoverished conception of pupils are members of a group new to schools: refugee children. These children have typically endured major personal traumas, yet are often without personal support of any kind, having entered the country unaccompanied. They will, almost always, have experienced major loss of some kind. For many, this will mean bereavement, for some, personal betrayal. They may have witnessed brutal and shocking events, may have seen their homes set alight by once-friendly neighbours. Their parents, if still around, are perhaps totally wrapped up in their own grief, only a shadow of the people they once were. Nor, for many such children, is their present home anything more than temporary and substandard accomodation.

Faced with the completely unknown world of school, these children are likely to feel wholly at a loss. Many will not have experienced schooling, many will know no English at all. Nor is school life just a matter of lessons; there are also the complex and amorphous break periods to be negotiated. In situations of such personal isolation, acute loneliness, as van Allen (1994) suggests, is probably the refugee child's only companion.

For these children their classroom teacher is often the sole caring person, the one adult able to offer comfort and support. And in many schools, teachers have somehow managed to rise to the huge challenge which this situation entails. Working collectively, sometimes supported by voluntary bodies outside education, groups of teachers have begun to evolve constructive and viable refugee policies. Carefully planned introductions to school, the development of appropriate teaching materials, the involvement of other pupils in befriending schemes; good practice is being gradually built up in a variety of schools, at both primary and secondary levels. But this is work against the grain: teachers' own insistence upon catering for a distinctive pupil group within a system which refuses to recognize or give priority to this kind of urgent educational need.

As Kelly insists, the basis of human development is socio-cultural. For Vygotsky also, learning and thinking are deeply and inextricably embedded in social relationships. And for Bruner too, educational progress takes place within the transactions of those who share a common culture. Yet the social relationships of school pupils are characteristically ignored and bypassed within a system which organizes children by age – and, increasingly, by academic ability. This becomes more and more the case at older levels. In most primary schools there is some room at least for informal talk between pupils, for joint projects and collaborative work. But at the secondary stage schooling becomes highly individualized, its goal solitary examination.

But though official organization may deny it, the character of classrooms remains unalterably social. The grouping of young people in ways that take no account of existing social patterns does not act to eliminate them. Among school pupils the web of social connection is subtle, complex, fluid – hardly encompassed by that global term, the peer group. However arbitrarily thrown together, children and young people make their own highly differentiated social positionings.

Social relationships are unsuppressible. The very vitality of pupils' interpersonal engagements ensures their continuity in even the most deadening of school surroundings. And these relations inform the stances which young people take within the schooling system. This influence goes beyond the undercover communications across the classroom between friends routinely separated during lessons. Nor is it just a matter of the essentially social reasons behind most option choices. The meaning of the social, for school pupils, is more even than its significance in encounters with the teacher: the importance or irrelevance of these encounters for other pupils, their interest, approval or disapprobation.

Social patterning amongst young people is not encompassed by a series of separate, individual relationships; of particular friendships and alliances, emnities and antagonisms. Children and young people have their own distinctive cultures. The task, for a new school entrant, is not only to acquire the pupil role, to master the procedural rules that govern formal educational transactions – the etiquette, as Mary Willes (1983) terms it, of classroom business. New pupils must also enter and establish some place for themselves within the cultural world of their peers. For many, this can mean the experience of suffering, of loneliness, fear and vulnerability.

In the school arena children do not meet each other as equals, but as social members already, and indelibly, differentiated by race, gender and social class – and perhaps also by disability. If the dimensions of dominance and inequality that operate in adult society also affect the interrelationships of children, this is hardly surprising. The young live their lives within a wider social world in which some are patently more equal than others.

Even at the earliest levels of education, unequal social power is visible in the encounters, the dealings of young children together. Even in the nursery, small girls and boys draw on superior physical strength or verbal skill to bully other children. For many boys, the transition to junior school seems to carry the sense of joining the 'male club', of beginning to belong to a tough macho world from which sad, fearful or tender feelings must be ruthlessly eliminated. And certainly in the later primary school girls are apt to feel excluded and devalued. This is not only because of boys' dominance of playground space. Unless there is a strong teacher-led culture to counter it, male pupils characteristically take over computers and other apparatus, and openly disparage girls' abilities. Nor is such treatment confined to girls. Despite the generally benign image of the primary schooling stage, widespread bullying and intimidation mean that for many children, their school lives are lived in a climate of fear. In the phrase coined by the Commission for Racial Equality (1987), some pupils learn in terror. Truancy, even school phobia, are far from rare reactions.

If the primary stage carries personal threats and dangers, these are likely to be multiplied in the transition to secondary school. Deprived of the emotional security, the solidarity of an established friendship group, young adolescent pupils face an alien, perhaps hostile cultural world. Those whose physical development is behind that of their peers – being generally undersized, not yet wearing a bra – can become the butt of cruel taunts. For girls, sexual harassment and physical assault are now real possibilities.

Among the dimensions which structure the social relationships of children and young people, that of race is both highly salient and very complex. Race is a lens through which, from an early age, school pupils view each other. This is illustrated by a recent study. Cecile Wright (1992) made detailed observations in three representative urban primary schools; in each school white children formed the majority. As Wright suggests, the significance of race is not always immediately obvious. A visitor in the classroom and playground would probably observe children working and playing, Black and White together. There would be few signs that 'race' figures significantly in their lives as children; the visitor would probably overhear no racist remarks or witness any other from of racist behaviour. It would be tempting to conclude that racism among children is not an issue that schools like these need to be concerned about.

Yet, as Wright argues, the evidence gathered in the study runs strongly counter to such a conclusion: 'On the contrary, it reveals that "race" and racism are significant features of the cultures of children in predominantly white primary schools' (p. 104). In these school cultures, as Wright goes on to show, the meaning of race is highly complicated. On the one hand, it entails physical harassment, the whole vocabulary of racist name-calling, the deprecation of minority cultural identities. But there is also another side:

> Friendship between black and white youth was extremely common and was grounded in an experience of being born and growing up through primary school in mixed working class neighbourhoods together, occupying the same recreational spaces, experiencing closely meshed life worlds and growing into adolescence with far more friendships and other network ties than had been true of their parents' generation. Secondly, black youth had been forging a distinctive and varied set of cultural practices that seemed to construct points of paradoxical access to whites.
>
> (*Wright, 1992, p. 105*)

The 'Leroy Syndrome', as this feature has been labelled, is still stronger at secondary level, where routine racist harassment stands alongside a white youth culture admiring and imitating many Afro-Caribbean cultural forms. This applies to the dialect used by Black young people, and also to the macho and sexist imagery of much rap music. Nor are personal and group relationships across racial lines any less complicated. Phil Cohen (1988), a particularly illuminating writer in this sphere, suggests that race takes its meaning for young people, not in isolation, but within the context of class and gender:

> Sexist imagery may at one moment add injury to racist insult, and in the next, unite White and Black boys in displays of male chauvinism; the shared experience of sexism may in one setting bring girls together, and in another polarise them through the operation of a racial double standard.
> (*Cohen, 1988, p. 78*)

If gender complicates the meaning of race in groupings of young people, social class forms a further element in the complex chemistry of social identity. As Cohen argues, class may often act to undermine educational attempts to deal with racism and sexism:

> The cultural negotiations amongst young people which both repro-duce *and* interrupt the links between racism and sexism often take place as part of a wider process of *class* resistance to the civilising mission of the school. In so far as educational interventions are made into these arenas they may well provoke a reaction which reinforces all the negative aspects of the school counter-culture.
> (*Cohen, 1988, p. 86*)

For many years head teachers and their staffs have been concerned to establish school communities in which all children are equally ac-knowledged, equally respected. But anti-racist and anti-sexist initiat-ives, or whole-school policies against bullying, cannot hope to get far without taking into account the existence and the strength of pupil cultures. Only by beginning to establish some negotiation, some dialogue, with the living, complex norms and values through which young people constitute their own social relations and practices, may it be possible to develop institutional cultures that are less oppressive.

Chapter 5

School Knowledge

In time there arise out there in the nowhere whole new cities, built outside the walls against which (the scientist) once leaned so confidently. Now his once 'perfect truths' tell him that what he can see is not so, and, faithful as he may try to be, he can offer no more than lip service to them. Now each time he looks up from his work and peers beyond his latest achievement, he wonders who he is to have imagined such things and what he is doing, and he shudders to think how much of his life was spent behind the old barriers, or what unseen walls may imprison him now. And then he wonders more: to what destinies has he been false – and why has the evening grown so late?
(*Kelly, 1978, p. 228*)

School knowledge is often portrayed as neutral and value-free. Yet what is offered from one generation to the next comes deeply imbued with cultural values; with the features that, in Howard Gardner's phrase, 'society has selected to honour, reward and cultivate' (Gardner and Perkins, 1989, p. 27). In the cultural climate of today, it is the National Curriculum which officially defines, as far as is possible, what should count as valued knowledge. Mathematics, English and science stand as its anchors, more peripheral spheres of knowing being history, geography, technology, art, music, religious education and modern languages.

When this curriculum was first presented, its educational goals were explicitly spelt out. These were, first, 'to prepare pupils for the responsibilities, opportunities and experiences of adult life', and second, 'to promote the moral and cultural development of pupils and society' (Department of Education and Science (1992) *The National Curriculum*, London, HMSO, p. 3). Probably few people involved in schooling would dispute these aims. They represent, in Kellyan language, widely agreed superordinate constructs, constructs which embody general governing values.

Large objectives such as these necessarily call for more than just the acquisition of a range of separate kinds of subject knowledge. If young people are to build constructive lives out of their classroom learning, the curriculum must somehow invest its ten subjects with far wider meanings than their most obvious, directly appreciable content. In part this is a matter of making links between different spheres of knowledge. And in this the National Curriculum, at least in principle, is conceived as an integrated whole.

From an early stage in the development of the new curriculum, relations between its subjects represented a focus of attention. The working groups charged with drawing up attainment targets and programmes of study were specifically asked to consider the links between their own and other subjects. Science, for instance, was defined as linked with mathematics, Design and Technology home economics, earth sciences and astronomy. In constructing common ground between these disparate areas of knowledge, broad themes could be developed. Pupils would be enabled to consider such questions as the use and misuse of energy, or the need for education in health and safety.

Work across the curriculum certainly carries rich possibilities for the extension of meaning. In Kellyan terms, it is thinking that crosses official boundaries – that makes connections between previously unrelated ideas – which is most likely to lead to new, wider dimensions of understanding. For many teachers such logic is self-evident. In primary schools, cross-curricular work has long been seen as a natural mode of learning. A typical local history project, for example, might draw upon mathematics and science as well as history. In investigating local changes in space, building use and pollution, pupils would make use of old maps, draw graphs and conduct surveys.

Primary level schooling does not of course allocate different subjects to different teachers. In itself, this avoids traditional barriers. And the relative pedagogic freedom which, at least until recently, primary teachers have enjoyed has made it easier for them to cut across conventional subject boundaries. Within a broadly Piagetian philosophy, work at this level of schooling has tended where possible to follow rather than dictate the direction of pupils' interests. And when children pursue their own real purposes, follow their own curiosity, they seldom stay within the narrow, ultimately arbitrary confines of particular school subjects.

The new demands of the National Curriculum – its requirements for specific subject teaching – may generally leave primary teachers less room for cross-curricular work. But in some spheres at least, the value of such work continues to be built in. A project at Key Stage 2 represents one example. This focuses on Benin, and includes material on its imperial history, its physical environment, its forms and techniques of art, its myths and oral history. As such, the work draws not just on history, but on geography, art, technology and English.

At secondary level, the retention of a cross-curricular emphasis may prove harder. For all its declared concern with links across subjects, the heavy overload which the new curriculum imposes may present major obstacles. Cross-curricular studies, where teachers establish them, lack the status and the resource backing of core and foundation subjects. Perhaps ultimately even more seriously, they are not subject to the validating power of the national assessment system.

Health education, environmental studies, economic and industrial awareness; many secondary teachers see these as vital classroom concerns. But determined efforts may be needed to retain them as more than mere add-ons to the official agenda of education. The marginalization of such spheres would of course mean a huge loss of learning potential. Subject boundaries are, in the end, matters of convenience. Their reification as fundamental delimitations of knowledge could only be, in Kelly's apt phrase, 'a hardening of the categories'.

Classroom learning contributes to the enlargement of young people's lives to the extent that it succeeds in offering 'really useful knowledge'. If cross-curricular work sometimes achieves this, it is because it entails broad concerns and understandings that can be directly related to pupils' lived experience. But there are other, perhaps occasional classroom breakthroughs that involve ostensibly quite didactic kinds of material. This happens when teaching enables children to make personal links between their own future lives and the traditional stuff of learning. Herbert Kohl (1971) provides an illustration in his account, *36 Children*. This short book describes Kohl's long-frustrated efforts to teach literacy to a class of alienated and recalcitrant boys. Only when at last, in exasperation, he began to argue the personal importance of this learning – its future value for their lives – did these boys' classroom stance become transformed.

Learning to read was suddenly no longer an imposition to be resisted. It had come to mean a real enlargement of their own life chances.

The conventions of learning and teaching tend to overlook the implicit values of classroom learning. English or science, mathematics or geography. They are often presented without any reference to their underlying significance – the reasons why, ultimately, they may be worth studying. Yet such meanings are typically far from self-evident. For many young people, the classroom curriculum carries no sense at all of personal relevance. For others, school subjects may be invested with meanings that are very different from the ones their teacher presupposes. This was certainly the case in a study of classroom collaboration which I carried out, together with Hilary Claire, some years ago (Salmon and Claire, 1984).

In exploring the perceptions of a second year class in design and technology, we compared their views of the subject with those of their teacher. Profound differences emerged. For the teacher, his curriculum entailed the development of designing capacity. He saw this as a process of imaginative construction and reconstruction; a process in which pupils could work collaboratively to try out ideas, compare notes and challenge each other. For him, the curriculum had room for personal creativeness, and was open to every pupil. In his perception, technical skills, and the particular artefact produced, were of secondary importance.

To the children in this teacher's class, their lessons in design and technology meant something very different. Almost universally they defined progression in the curriculum in terms of the artefact produced. They saw learning as developing from 'make-believe', 'practice' objects, such as model bridges, to objects that were usable and 'for real', such as shelves. This valuation stood in direct opposition to the teacher's priorities, which set the imaginative power needed to construct a model bridge well above the purely mechanical skills involved in making a simple shelf.

The design and technology workshop, for these children, was a kind of assembly plant in miniature. They did not see their work within it as creative, judging technical skills to be of paramount importance. In line with this perception, the learning process was seen as one of individual effort and practice, rather than involving collaboration with other pupils. And most children, far from seeing learning as open to all, viewed competence as largely inborn, with female gender being an insuperable barrier.

This kind of material seems important. As Kelly insists, we all read situations according to the meaning we give them, the interpretation we make about them. To the pupils in this particular class group, their classroom learning meant something very different from the meaning with which their teacher invested it. They read their own significance into what they were asked to do; they judged the success, the progress of their work in their own, different terms and by their own criteria. To this extent, despite the generally positive classroom atmosphere, teacher and pupils were largely bypassing each other.

This particular teacher chose to make these disjunctions of perception the focus of class discussion. This proved educationally fruitful. When teachers bring into classroom discourse the ramifications of school learning – its wider meanings, its underlying significance – the outcomes are often valuable. In Kellyan logic, it is through exploring the whole network of connotations that surround ideas that new personal meanings may be achieved.

The rhetoric which frames the National Curriculum is universal. Every child is to benefit from school learning, every young life to be enhanced. But, as is all too clearly documented, our schooling system acts, however inadvertently, to disadvantage certain pupils. This phenomenon is likely to become more, rather than less evident in the present culture of market forces. Where schools are forced into competition through the operation of league tables, certain groups of pupils will certainly suffer. Not merely those with 'special needs', but children who are in any way 'different' must inevitably represent unwelcome classroom members.

The school curriculum has itself also contributed to the sense of exclusion which many pupils have experienced. Its cultural narrowness has carried messages, for minority groups, of being marginalized – of being placed, perhaps with a patronizing nod of acknowledgement, on the sidelines of human life. At its worst, classroom learning has contained no echo, for such pupils, of their familiar lives, their felt identities. In the words of Adrienne Rich, 'When someone with the authority of a teacher describes the world and you are not in it, there is a moment of psychic disequilibrium, as if you looked into a mirror and saw nothing' (Rich, 1989).

For many concerned teachers, early versions of the new curriculum aroused anxieties that similar kinds of cultural exclusivity were again to be built in. From the Eurocentric canon of English texts to the dominance of Christianity in religious education, the norms and ways of life of minority groups seemed to be bypassed. Active professional protest has, of course, done much to widen these limits. Not merely has the conception of many subjects become broadened – allowing history teachers, for example, to include in their curriculum discussion of human rights and world inequalities. Beyond this, it has proved feasible to retain pioneering anti-racist and non-sexist teaching within the programmes of study for science and mathematics.

Promoting the moral development of pupils and society; that is one of the two fundamental aims of the new curriculum. And probably no one involved in schooling would deny that our present social order is deeply flawed by injustice, inequality and oppression. Over recent years many teachers at all educational levels have striven to put such issues on the educational agenda. In much current educational practice, the raising of awareness about race and racism, gender and sexism, have become an established part of classroom work. These are seen by those involved as representing one route into political consciousness, and perhaps ultimately to changes in social practices.

Although there are probably rather few teachers who follow the debating methods of Lawrence Stenhouse, nevertheless verbal discussion of some kind is likely to form the currency of these kinds of learning enterprise. Yet, as Kelly believed, our most important constructions are often unavailable to consciousness, and therefore to explicit verbalization.

If pupils are to contemplate the social problems in which they, like all of us, are implicated, they need first to articulate and then to begin to question how they understand their own everyday lives, their own cultural practices. It is popular culture which underpins social life, which informs and supports the ways we go about things together. It represents the whole network of inexplicit and taken-for-granted constructions through which we actually live. Bruner, like Kelly, sees this 'folk psychology' as fundamentally important: 'The folk psychology of ordinary people is not just a set of self-assuaging illusions, but the cultural beliefs and working hypotheses about what makes it possible and fulfilling for people to live together, even with great personal sacrifice' (Bruner, 1990, p. 106).

To take this logic seriously means that somehow the curriculum of education has to be brought into real connection with the street knowledge of children and young people. Rather than remaining abstract and unrelated, school lessons must make links with pupils' own implicit psychologies, their tacit sociological understandings.

Young people's sense of right and wrong, of what is ordinary and unexceptionable, their intuitive feelings of identity and otherness; something of this needs to be articulated, made visible.

In a project entitled Dimensions of Childhood, Lesley Smith (1988) built up a curriculum for 16 plus education which embodied these principles. Rather than studying a set course in child development, these learners were invited to consider their own childhoods, and those of others, in terms of six dimensions: race, gender, worldwide, socio-economic, historical and hidden. The curriculum was essentially non-didactic. Instead, it involved young people in examining the personal and social meaning of these dimensions within their own and others' lives. The materials were visual as well as verbal, and lent themselves to experiential work.

As the evaluator of this study, I saw something of its working out and its outcomes. What was particularly impressive was the highly personal learning which it typically brought about. The adolescent men and women who engaged with these educational materials did so, necessarily, from within their own intuitive frames of reference; their personal construct systems. But in beginning to articulate these personal understandings, these learners gained for themselves a clearer, wider view. It is not easy to put our deepest meanings into verbal formulation, to make them accessible to ourselves and others. But if we are able to do this, we gain real personal insight; the ability to reflect upon some of the assumptions we live by.

Race and gender, these are hardly unfamiliar aspects of the lives of today's young people. Yet living amongst the social meanings of these categories does not make them available to conscious reflection, let alone to deliberate personal intention. Like the epochal themes of Paolo Freire, these social dimensions have a hugely powerful impact on all those in our society. And by the same Freirean logic, it is the capacity to grasp for oneself – to be able to put into words something of their lived meaning – which allows an enlargement of one's own social agency.

The success of this project – conducted outside the curricular constraints of most school learning – was almost certainly related to its pedagogic modes. Non-verbal materials, the use of images: these are perhaps particularly fertile in eliciting responses from highly personal, deeply intuitive levels of understanding. Trying too soon to find words for something felt but not yet known, can often drive it into inaccessibility. Only after it has been anchored within a visual form, can efforts to give it clear verbal formulation be valuable.

There is surely another reason why visual modes are likely to be fruitful at this level of education. A virtually universal visual literacy, in the worlds of television, computers and computer games, allows children and young people to move about the world of images with freedom and confidence. Those who may in classroom learning seem quite unacademic are typically intelligent and sophisticated in these familiar modes. Young people who can barely read, for instance, are often easily able to 'read' the language of fast-moving images in programmes that may be beyond many adults' comprehension.

In this medium, young people sometimes create their own spontaneous kinds of discourse analysis. Who made this programme? Aimed at whom? What message? In whose interests? To pupils for whom an entirely verbal context might pose difficulties, such questions, vital to a serious consideration of social issues, often come quite naturally.

As many teachers have shown, media studies – now relegated to a minor part of the English curriculum – can provide an ideal route into the exploration of personal and social understanding. Such natural modes allow young people to begin to grapple with issues of social relationships, of social power and control, of competing ideologies. Where it has been possible to provide pupils with video cameras, learning can progress still further. As is clear from the studies of Phil Cohen (1987), when young people come to represent their own social worlds, they not only articulate their understandings; they start to question previously taken-for-granted cultural realities.

But all this lies a long way from the formal curriculum, even in its rethought version. Built into most school knowledge are deeply entrenched positivistic assumptions. Behind the new curriculum, as John Eliot (1991) argues, is the assumption that subjects are essentially repositories of factual knowledge, and that values lie outside their scope, being a matter of purely private preference. On this assumption, the acquisition of knowledge is seen as quite separate from the problems of everyday living. The first is the proper business of schooling; the second is not.

As Eliot argues, it is in the interests of a state-controlled curriculum to produce individuals who will be 'smoothly functioning economic units' (Eliot, 1991, p. 42) Moral complexities can only be disfunctional to this aim. So the curriculum must avoid the acknowledgement of conflicting social norms and interests. In attending merely to the process of knowledge acquisition, classroom learning can focus the attention of pupils on to 'facts' – the surface appearances of things.

Yet the refusal to question 'facts', so far from leading to intellectual advancement, is stultifying. Edward Said, a writer himself well used to controversy, believes that people defined as intellectuals have a duty to ask embarrassing questions. True thinkers are those who 'confront othodoxy and dogma, rather than producing them, who cannot easily be co-opted by governments or corporations, and whose *raison d'être* is to represent all those people and issues who are routinely forgotten or swept under the mat' (Said, 1993, p. 3).

A schooling which does no more than confirm and elaborate taken-for-granted realities of common sense is not likely to produce significant educational development. The mere reproduction of consensus truths is not enough. As Kelly puts it: 'While a common or similar cultural background tends to make people see things alike and behave alike, it does not guarantee cultural progress' (1955, p. 206). It is through questioning, challenging, problematizing conventional understandings that real learning, and ultimately new human possibilities, may come about. Educational materials which show diverse and conflicting meanings, which portray the cultural complexity of our world; these are much more likely to provoke real debate, real thinking, than those which show pupils only a bland and unreal homogeneity. If multicultural education benefits all children, not just those from cultural minority groups, it is because meeting other ways of seeing, of valuing, of living, is itself a powerful stimulus to thought.

Chapter 6

Learning and Not Learning

> It is possible to restate many of the achievements of man in terms of the logic we have so far formalised. But this does not tell us much about how the achievements came about. Nor does it help at all in finding how to disengage ourselves from the logic by which those achievements are presently sustained so we can go on to greater ones. For example, most of our formalised logic has to do with the establishment of certainties. But human progress depends also upon the selective creation of uncertainties; that is to say, the pinpointing of preposterous doubts and the formulation of new questions and issues.
> (*Maher, 1969, p. 114*)

Between the ages of seven and ten years I was unable to master the telephone. I could not tell which end was which, and so it was always a matter of chance which piece I put to my mouth and which to my ear. As I had to use the telephone at home once a week to arrange a lesson with a local violin teacher, I regularly experienced the shame of my very visible incompetence being witnessed by the five other children in my family, whose scorn, disbelief or kindly rescue were the usual sequel to my attempts at telephoning.

In those days, the earpiece and mouthpiece of telephones were more clearly differentiated than they are nowadays. There was certainly nothing wrong with my eyesight; I was good at jigsaw puzzles, and I had a collection of very small china animals whose tiny details I often dwelt on. And there must have been many times when my aunt, with patience and love, tried to help me connect the different shapes of the receiver with where I should put them – as well as the frequent, often exasperated instructions of the other children. Yet despite my adequate perceptual equipment and the teaching I received, I could not, over several years, acquire this piece of learning.

I now think the reason I could not learn to use the telephone properly was that what I already knew about myself completely ruled out the possibility of learning it. When it came to sports, physical or practical skills, finding your way about places or knowing where things were kept: in all these areas I was stupid and incompetent. I was stupid, and I was known to be stupid. Because of this, nothing that could have increased my competence was able to register with me. I do not think I really saw the telephone receiver clearly, or actually heard the helpful things people told me. I just experienced, time after time, the same sickening, miserable anticipation that yet again I was going to show myself up – and that is what always happened.

Some years later, when I was about 15, I had begun to enjoy playing the piano. One day my school music teacher decided that I should learn a piece by Beethoven. The piece she chose was a bagatelle, which technically was easier than some of the other pieces I could play. But when I tried to learn it, I seemed unable to master it. I could not get the notes or the rhythm quite right, and I felt somehow that I was unable to interpret the music. My teacher endorsed these feelings by eventually declaring that I had better drop the attempt to learn the piece, and adding that perhaps, after all, Beethoven 'wasn't my composer'.

This judgement made me rather sad, but it did not entirely surprise me. I was familiar with several Beethoven symphonies, and loved them. I also knew and liked some of Beethoven's piano music; but this was almost entirely through hearing it played by my cousin Stephen, who played virtually no other composer. Somehow this made Beethoven's piano music his. The sonatas and bagatelles belonged to Stephen, and that meant that I had no right to the music. There was no question of his objecting to my learning something by Beethoven; yet I knew that I was not entitled to it. In one sense, I suppose, I had the knowledge, the capacity to play Beethoven; but I was not free to draw upon that knowledge, because I could not feel it to be mine. This had to do with family boundaries of personal identity, which defined what kinds of orientations and understandings one could and could not claim for oneself.

In a perspective which views knowledge as something separate from the sense of self, these kinds of failure to learn look merely perverse, perhaps even wanton. If there is opportunity, motivation and encouragement, and the absence of any real disability, then surely there can be no reason *not* to learn? For a traditional understanding, learning experiences such as these are difficult to explain.

Yet school classrooms offer daily examples of knowledge which inexplicably fails to take. In her mathematics class, the teacher, with several examples, explains the rule for converting decimals into fractions. As the pupils begin working on their exercises, she notices one girl getting things badly wrong. Quietly she takes her through the correct procedure, wording it differently this time, and illustrating with the exercise the girl has attempted. But, encouraged to try the next, this pupil shows that she is still totally at sea. Why this block, wonders her teacher, knowing the girl to be both able and conscientious in her general schoolwork, and having witnessed her facility with numbers in the nearby sweet shop.

In personal construct psychology, learning is not an intellectual game played at a distance, but a revision of one's very self. For what we know, we know in the end about ourselves. When particular ways of knowing, particular stances towards the world, feel somehow at odds with one's own familiar positions, they cannot be taken on. Knowledge which cannot be fitted into personal identity must be ruled out.

Identity, as Kelly insisted, is forged out of interaction with others. Who we are is inextricably bound up with who we are known to be. Children bring to school very particular family identities, identities which facilitate some kinds of learning, but inhibit others. Social relationships with other young people, and participation in school culture, act to produce new dimensions in the sense of self, which frame the meaning of pupils' classroom conduct, and closely govern what they may and may not do.

Some school identities embody positions which are fundamentally hostile to the educational establishment. The 'lads', for example, in Paul Willis' influential study, *Learning to Labour* (1977), maintained their proudly guarded school reputations by seeking constantly to distance themselves from official schooling, and from the 'ear-oles' who were aligned with it. This entailed using every possible opportunity for showing disrespect towards classroom learning, and for undermining the authority of school and teachers.

The boys whom Willis studied formed part of a well-established counter-culture. Within their lives as young working class men, this stance made its own kind of sense, and had continuity, as the book illustrates, with the one they later came to adopt in the world of work. To many teachers, especially at secondary level, this stance is all too easily recognizable. The low academic achievement with which it is typically associated is all part of the picture. For many young people, their own alienation from school comes to be reciprocally endorsed by its explicit or covert judgements of their educational inadequacy.

Being a pupil means being judged. As Philip Jackson (1968) argued many years ago, constant exposure to official evaluation is one of the dimensions fundamentally defining life in classrooms. Even at infant level, children are aware of teachers' judgements, and understand something of where they personally stand. As they get older, pupils become experts in knowing the hierarchy, and typically see through efforts at disguising this.

Built into one's sense of oneself, feelings of incompetence become self-fulfilling prophecies. My own early ineptitude with the telephone is one example. And school learning is of course full of others. The effects of labelling are only too well known. Global judgements of academic inadequacy act to ensure its perpetuation. Being found wanting in a particular area will very likely mean, in the words of Guy Claxton (1984, p. 214), 'filing that sphere of learning under school, and sealing it off for ever'.

Evaluation in some form is intrinsic to an educational system. But contemporary political pressures have tended to force this away from sensitive, formative assessments, and into a series of hard and fast judgements within a standardized and often arbitrary scale. For many pupils, this means a public record of academic inadequacy. Examinations in particular may act to crystallize blocks in learning, and may, as Frank Huggett suggests, 'have repercussions 15, 20, 30 years later. Exams are cruel statements which make judgements which remain with people for ever' (Huggett, 1986, p. 107).

Teachers themselves are of course much concerned to avoid terminal judgements of failure, and typically act to mitigate the effects of these experiences. Yet while it is sometimes possible to avoid the sense of academic inferiority which so effectively disables learning, there are other, less obvious aspects of identity which can be equally inhibiting. My efforts at learning a Beethoven bagatelle came to grief, not through a feeling of pianistic inadequacy, but out of an intuitive sense that such music could somehow never be mine.

The psycho-logic of learning draws its own lines of demarcation. Knowledge is not free-standing or disembodied. Particular spheres of knowing *belong*; belong to particular concerns, particular lifestyles, particular kinds of people. For every pupil, some of the knowledge which schooling presents is vested in socio-cultural groups that are 'other'. One central dimension of this otherness is of course gender. As perhaps the most fundamental identity of all, being male or female rules out certain kinds of knowledge, just as it leads easily, naturally, into others that are felt to be one's own by right.

The history of anti-sexist work in schools has entailed a growing awareness of the subtlety and the complexity of the process whereby school knowledge comes to be framed by gender. This is not just a matter of the typically male teachers of mathematics or science, nor even of the ways in which even apparently neutral subjects become gender-typed. There are also crucial messages in teachers' unintended but differential attention to their male and female pupils, and in the multiple and subtle ways in which the language of sex and gender regulates behaviour and expectations within the classroom. Increasingly, teachers' strategies have encompassed an attention to the less overt, but perhaps ultimately more significant aspects of sexism in school learning.

Most accounts of education portray knowledge and its acquisition in terms that are quite straightforward. Yet learning and not learning are very complicated matters. For it is possible to know and not know at the same time; for construct systems, in Kelly's terminology, to be fragmented. Some years ago, David Hargreaves (1977) gave a group of 10-year-old boys and girls a drawing task, the Circles Test, in which there are characteristic differences in the performance of the two genders. After these children had done the test, Hargreaves asked them to do it again, but this time pretending to be someone of the opposite sex. Sure enough, girls drew objects typical of boys' productions, while boys drew those characteristic of girls. Girls, it seems, know how to be boys, and boys, how to be girls.

This apparently paradoxical situation is not confined to the context of gender. In a still more remarkable experiment, which he called 'Imagine you're clever', Robert Hartley (1986) invited disadvantaged 7- and 8-year-olds to perform the same test twice, acting on the second occasion as 'someone who is very very clever'. The test, a favourite in children's comics, required the matching of a figure with one of a series of slightly different alternatives.

Under these conditions, children whose performance, as 'themselves', had been classified as impulsive, produced reponses that were clearly reflective. Instead of approaching the matching task in a rapid and imprecise way, when 'being clever' they showed caution, deliberation, and a marked concern for accuracy. These outcomes show that even such supposedly fixed parameters as cognitive ability may be a product of the roles which, as particular kinds of people, we habitually take.

When Hartley told these children's teachers the results of his experiment, their reaction was one of pleased surprise. But merely knowing of this unexpected intellectual potential did not enable them to transform their pupils' classroom learning. Over the following weeks these boys and girls continued to behave in their accustomed ways, living out their role as disadvantaged pupils.

In Kelly's terms, to act out of character, to abandon the personal identity, the core role which gives coherence and integrity to our living: this is the ultimate human threat. 'Faced with the stark realisation that we are on the brink of a changed outlook, of an imminent comprehensive change in one's core structures', we draw back. To enact another kind of character, to behave differently under the declared rubric of pretence, is not necessarily threatening. But stepping right outside our own established identity, into conduct in which we feel ourselves to be unrecognizable: that is another matter altogether.

Learning probably always involves some degree of threat. In coming to see things differently we have to give up the security, the comfortableness, of what we thought we knew. This involves an acknowledgement of our own present incompetence, a sense of vulnerability, loss of safety and exposure. Even if there are no intimidatory pressures, no risks of ridicule or humiliation, learning carries, at least for a time, the experience of personal confusion, of floundering, of feeling at sea. And that itself may lead learners to lose heart. Kelly writes:

> Almost everything new starts in some moment of confusion. But this is not to say that confusion always serves to produce something new. It can just as well have the opposite effect, especially if the person finds the confusion so intolerable that he reverts to some older interpretation of what is going on.
> (*Maher, 1969, p. 151*)

Successful learning situations are those which, by supporting learners, enable them to tolerate some measure of anxiety. Perhaps this means, more than anything, the ability to create psychological space.

In struggling towards new understandings, people who are learning need a sort of temporary moratorium, a distance between themselves and their present efforts, a suspension of being called to account. Real learning, as Kelly insists, is an essentially creative endeavour. Reconstruction 'arises out of preposterous thinking'; it is killed by 'the notion that we ought always to be right before we commit ourselves, a notion that later makes it very hard to concede our mistakes, or revise our construction of the world' (Maher, 1969, p. 150).

Personal construct psychology lays stress on the ability to try things out, to think in hypothetical and provisional ways. We learn, not by seeking to find some absolute truth, but by exploring where ideas lead – what might follow from a particular way of seeing things. Bruner argues a similar case. Learning, he believes, does not happen if we ask only whether a particular view is or is not correct. Rather it proceeds from asking 'What would it be like to believe that? and what would I be committing myself to if I believed that?' (Bruner, 1990, p. 92).

The remarkable outcomes of Hargreaves' and Hartley's experiments seem to have come about because both experimental situations freed children from the usual constraints of being themselves. Similarly adventurous breakthroughs regularly occur, of course, in drama, English or history lessons which engage children in role playing. In these situations, too, pupils are able to try out a new way of seeing and doing things, at a kind of psychological distance. Without forcing too public a personal acknowledgement of such knowledge – too early or too explicit a personal owning of it – teachers can then act to affirm its general validity.

In other areas of the school curriculum, it is often less easy to find ways of facilitating hypothetical thinking. Where knowledge is presented in literal, right-or-wrong terms, children cannot easily disengage from habitual responses, or find the confidence to be tentative, to try things out for themselves. Nor do such approaches lend themselves to teachers' delicate negotiation with existing understanding, without which no learning can occur. For of course children are not empty vessels, and no pupil ever enters ignorant into a new sphere of knowledge.

Thanks to the insights of Jean Piaget, even very young children are now seen as making sense. Where once the responses of 5-year-olds, their 'wrong' answers to questions, were classified as simple cognitive incompetence, they are now viewed as expressing a different kind of understanding. The perceptions, the reasoning of a child at the pre-operational stage of thought has its own distinctive logic: not that of the concrete or the formal operational stages, but logic just the same. To an adult and a child of two the same situation may look different; but to each, things add up in their own particular way.

As many teachers see it, curricular knowledge has to be anchored within children's existing ways of seeing things. Only if understandings are connected with what is already meaningful – and interesting – to pupils, may they translate into usable meanings. A study carried out some years ago by Estelle Phillips (1982) illustrates one attempt to achieve this.

In this study, Phillips worked with a design and technology teacher concerned to open up his curriculum to a first year secondary group. The class was mixed, and it included some pupils who had done primary work in craft, along with others who had not. Each child was asked to think about a list of 12 manufactured objects: a saw, a bicycle, a Marmite jar, a plastic toy duck, a brick, and so on. Considering these items in successive triads, the pupils were invited to put two together, apart from the third. They worked their way through six such triads, writing down the similarity and difference for each in turn. Their individual judgements were then put up on the board, and the class discussed them.

This material proved both unexpected and fascinating to the pupil group. Not everyone, it was evident, made the same kind of sense of their common experience. For a boy to whom the saw and the bicycle were alike because they were made of metal, as against the glass of the Marmite jar, his classmate's comparison of transparent versus opaque came as a surprise. Different meanings also emerged out of dissimilar contrasts. To one child, ornamental might be contrasted with ugly; to another, with useful.

Commonalities of perception also became apparent. Some of these were related to gender, girls tending to use aesthetic dimensions of comparison as against boys' typically functional ones. It was clear, too, that previous experience of craft lessons created common ground. Those who had shared this experience, even though this had been in different schools, tended to use some similar categorizations.

On one level all this is unsurprising. Given the task involved, one might expect that children's construing of manufactured objects would be partly similar, partly dissimilar, and that both gender and previous classroom experience might influence perceptions. Yet making this material explicit – making it the focus of reflection and discussion – helped children articulate and think about the implicit basis of this learning sphere. The exercise allowed both the pupils and their teacher to acknowledge that there are many ways of looking at the world of manufactured objects. It gave rise to an understanding that gender may influence how people see this world. It also allowed a discussion of the fact that the design and technology curriculum entails its own specialized perceptions, some of these quite like those already available to children, others more remote.

This kind of exercise – comparable with many that teachers themselves devise – locates school learning within the existing personal psychology of learners. Its way of engaging children recognizes that they already possess their own kind of sense of the materials of the curriculum. And by making this explicit, it demonstrates something of the relation between everyday understandings and official school knowledge. In Margaret Donaldson's (1978) phrase, it makes vital links between 'human sense' and the more abstract sense of the educational curriculum.

In considering triads of objects, the pupils in this exercise drew upon their own personal constructs, their own dimensions of meaning. Learning, as the elaboration of meaning, entails changes in the relations between constructs. This is not, of course, a simple incremental process. Coming to a new understanding necessarily involves a period of disequilibrium; a disrupting of previously established connections, followed by a time of confusion before a new kind of equilibrium is found.

Significant alterations in construing are, in Kelly's terms, not merely those of slot change – simple reversals of meaning. This would only entail viewing things as opposite to the way one had seen them before. Rather they demand shift change; the drawing on different constructs, meanings which have not been used before within this area of construing. Change of this order is much more complicated, involving a different perspective altogether. And this is not achieved within an all-at-once discovery, but represents a wayward, difficult process, full of blind alleys, in which various ways of looking at things must be tried out before, perhaps, something satisfying emerges.

Just how complicated real learning may be is illustrated by an American study of practising teachers, carried out many years ago by Philip Runkel and Dora Damrin (1961). Working with secondary teachers, they invited judgements about a series of imaginary school problems. This task allowed an assessment of the simplicity or complexity of the way in which teachers viewed such problems. At the simplest level, a teacher might reduce a whole series of problems down to one single common category. At the most complex, each problem would be seen as entirely different from every other.

Runkel and Damrin compared three groups of teachers, in terms of the length of their professional training: elementary, intermediate and advanced. What emerged from this comparison was at first sight quite paradoxical. The relation between level of training and complexity of construing was not linear, but curvilinear. Teachers with as yet only minimal training characteristically operated quite a complex view of school problems. The next stage, however, was associated with a markedly simpler way of seeing things. Finally at the third, most advanced level of training, most teachers had again adopted a highly complex view.

These findings seem to challenge many of the ways in which we usually think about learning. Certainly they cannot be fitted into an additive model. If prolonged educational development simply meant quantitative growth, then construing would just get steadily more complex. But even with a qualitative view of change – a view which sees it as arriving at different kinds of understanding – it is hard at first sight to make sense of this kind of progression. How could teachers undergoing further professional training come to adopt a simpler construction than those at a less advanced training stage? Doesn't learning entail the realization that things are *more*, rather than *less* complicated than we had previously thought?

In order to understand this apparently paradoxical finding, we have to look to the ways in which people test out what they think they know. It was Piaget, again, who insisted on the need for learners to make constant reference to the external world; on his argument, we must continually rework the balance between assimilation and accomodation. In this, it is crucial to experience the non-viability of our existing understanding.

In the process of struggling with some difficult problem, we seem suddenly to get it. But then we find, to our dismay, that it does not work. Our seeming solution does not, after all, give us the necessary leverage on what is going on, to grasp what is essentially involved, to anticipate how things will actually turn out. Yet this experience of failure is itself essential. It is, most fundamentally, the *unsuccessful* outcomes of putting our understanding to the test which takes the learning endeavour further. Disconfirmation of what we expected is crucial to development. In Kellyan terminology, invalidation is the key to reconstruction.

In a Year 6 mathematics lesson observed by Sheila Macrae (1994), pupils were invited to work on palindromic numbers. Having provided one demonstration of the procedure, their teacher asked them to see if they could discover any patterns, any rules. Trying out various possibilities, several pupils proudly announced that they had 'cracked it', only to find, through the teacher's further questions, that they had not actually solved the problem at all. Because the task, for this class, was challenging and intriguing, these young people continued to work things out for themselves, their mistaken thinking proving an impetus to further thought rather than a 'failure'.

Applied to the study of Runkel and Damrin, this logic suggests that professional learning also entails qualitatively discrete stages. Those teachers who had reached an advanced stage of their training must have passed through the kinds of thinking characteristic of earlier stages. They had presumably begun, in initial training, by seeing school problems and their resolution as no simple matter. If during further training they reduced their construing to a crudely simplistic level, it was because only then could they clearly test it out. If they later proceeded to build a more complicated view for themselves, this was because the validational outcomes of their simplified understanding had shown it to be inadequate – to require further elaboration. Only then was it possible to build such a view, since now there existed at least a rudimentary foundation.

Such changes may also be seen as involving the growth of confidence towards an area of understanding. As teachers in training become more confident in themselves, they may come to feel that things are actually simpler than they had previously believed. Experience then throws spanners in the works, by showing that matters are not so easily understood. But by this stage, the teachers are able to accept such disconfirmation, because they have developed a sense of being able to cope, a conviction of potential personal understanding.

Sudden apparent revelations, in the struggle to achieve new understanding, are probably a vital stage. Typically they turn out to be false. Yet for all their disappointment, they allow real engagement, out of which further thinking may come.

A Kellyan perspective on learning does not view it as a simple process. Its highly personal character makes it a delicate plant to nurture. Yet it is the same personal character which gives it, potentially, its inspiration and excitement. For when classroom learning does catch fire, it is not only through its connections with what is already known and accepted. On those rare occasions when the material of education reaches into pupils' core constructions, then learning can become an act of love, to which young people bring passion and intensity of purpose.

Chapter 7

The Construction of 'Difference'

> John is a patient, a very sick one, who needs professional care. And if he is sick we are all sick and we had better turn ourselves in for treatment. If we are not too resistant to our psychoanalysts we may eventually be able to hobble around on our own, but every day we must remember who our masters are and make the necessary concession to keep peace with them.
> (*Maher, 1969, p. 343*)

Idiot, moron, moral imbecile, educationally subnormal, juvenile delinquent, personality disorder, maladjusted, mental or physical handicap, behaviour problem, slow learner, children with special needs. Over the years each term has chased out the other in a vain attempt to escape the stigma of being 'different'. For ours is a society which, as Harold Rosen (1993) argues, cannot conceive of diversity except as deviance or maladjustment.

Brought into general currency through the Warnock Report and the 1981 Act which followed it, the term special need seemed at first to promise another way; a vision of educational difficulties which did not pathologize them. For need was both more broadly defined than by previous labels, and, still more crucially, conceived as integral with provision. One in every six; surely that many children could not be viewed as so very different? And if having special needs meant merely access to extra educational provision, then surely it could not carry the traditional connotations of being beyond the schooling pale?

This nomenclature introduced a new view of educational difficulties; one which defined problems as lying *between* rather than *within*. Its focus was no longer on individualized pathology, but on the relation between particular pupils and their school settings. If wheel-chaired children cannot be accommodated in ordinary schools – so might run the argument – this is because these institutions do not provide the necessary ramps and lifts, and have thereby created their own mobility barriers. If some pupils prove impossibly restless in class, this arises out of the routine insistence that lively, physically ebullient young people must sit quietly at their desks for long periods at a stretch. If children of limited academic ability cannot be fitted into the classroom, this calls into question the school's mixed ability policy. And truancy and school phobia could be seen as reactions to school settings which are large, frightening and insensitive.

From this viewpoint, most educational problems could be solved by the provision of further resources, so that integration, for almost every child, became a reality. Tutorial support could be made regularly available for pupils with serious academic difficulties. Visual aids and sign language interpreters would be there for those with sensory deficits. For second language learners, there could be mother tongue teaching and two-way translation of texts and worksheets.

What has happened to this generous logic? In current educational realities it is hard to recognize. So far from moving to enlarge their learning opportunities, to make room for a wider pupil constituency, mainstream schools, at the mercy of crude performance indicators, are increasingly forced into the use of exclusion. To school managers, a high proportion of special needs pupils may seem likely to prove a disincentive to prospective middle class parents, even to contribute to a reputation as a 'sink' school. Ironically, good special needs provision may seem to carry similar dangers, so that some schools actually run down their own successful units.

A growing number of children, relegated to Pupil Referral Units, have, in the words of Paul Cooper and his colleagues, 'dropped off the edge of the known world' (Cooper *et al.*, 1994, p. 49). Effectively losing entitlement to the National Curriculum, taught by staff who themselves lack financial and professional support, these young people have little chance of re-entering mainstream schooling, and are often merely contained until they reach school-leaving age.

The concept of special need is itself more often associated with segregated than with integrated schooling; statementing procedures seldom bring mainstream schools the educational support services they require. Its original inclusion of gifted pupils is long forgotten; the term is now equated with failure to come up to the mark. Somehow, like all their predecessors, *special* and *need* have turned out weasel words. So far from signifying belonging and entitlement, these terms have themselves become typically divisive, with connotations of helplessness and inadequacy justifying segregation. The concept of special need has failed to revolutionize the treatment of educational difference, and is often used to denote the very thing against which it once protested: individualized pathology.

Kellyan psychology lays its most fundamental importance on personal constructs. As we construe a situation, so we construct our practices within it. If the increasing trend towards stigmatizing certain groups of pupils is to be halted, we have to look with the very greatest care at the words we use – the dimensions of meaning which underlie how things become organized.

Failure, disorder, deficit; these words clearly locate educational difficulties within individual children. On the one hand, they justify exclusion and relegate the problem to a specialist, often pseudo-medical expertise. By the same token, they leave teachers feeling helpless and deskilled. But beyond this, such labels also convey an impasse; they carry no clues as to possible strategies or ways forward.

The concept of special need, at least in its original connotation, was concerned not with individual attributes but with interaction; interaction between school pupils and their educational settings. If failure was to be defined at all, it was likely to be the school failing the pupil, rather than the other way round. The emphasis was on the necessity for the system to meet the needs of the child.

Yet need, as many writers have insisted, is a deeply problematic concept. Ostensibly benevolent, it nevertheless glosses over crucial issues of value and of power. Applied to pupils in the institution of school, it presupposes a universal agreement between all those involved. It disguises the fact that what is defined as need has not been negotiated with children themselves or their parents. In this way, the norms and values of an educational establishment become directly translated into something that all children apparently 'need'.

> Framing professional judgments in terms of children's needs serves to direct attention away from the particular adult position from which they are made. Projected onto children themselves, they acquire spurious objectivity. In this way, cultural prescriptions for childhood are presented as if they were intrinsic qualities of children's own psychological make-up.
> (*Woodhead, 1993, p. 45*)

Whose interests are actually served by the separate forms of education to which special need categorization generally leads? Those at the receiving end – pupils and their families – often feel unhappy with such provision. Even where there are specialist staff and facilities, unavailable in mainstream schools, such privileged access is typically outweighed by the stigma with which it is inextricably invested.

As long as a decade ago, when many people were still hopeful about special education, it seemed that specialized provision carried its own problems. Discussing priority admission to preschool nursery education, Patricia Potts wrote:

> It can be argued that the priority system ensures that those who need the provision most get a place. The trouble is that children with special needs who enter on a priority ticket can still be seen as second class citizens. Identifying groups of children as 'disadvantaged', even if this is a prelude to positive discrimination, can only be socially divisive. (*Potts, 1984, p. 5*)

Looked at in abstract terms, there seems no reason why difference, in educational forms, should mean inferiority. To be able to read braille is surely an educational achievement in its own right, no less impressive than the use of visual modes. Yet, as spokesmen for the disabled have eloquently argued, it is the social restrictions and hostile attitudes they encounter which essentially render their conditions so disabling.

In their study, *The Politics of Mental Handicap*, Joanna Ryan and Frank Thomas (1980) documented the daily lives of people living in a hospital for the mentally handicapped. Underlying the definition of deficiency, as they tellingly show, are certain normative assumptions. Essentially, these embody a valuation of human life only in so far as it fits closely into the competitive individualism of a capitalist economy. Within these terms, people who do not take their place as 'productive' members of society are deemed inadequate.

As part of the wider society, our educational system necessarily carries and reproduces, at least in part, dominant social values. Given the massive political intervention of recent years, the gearing of schooling to the narrowly defined needs of the economy has inevitably gained ground. A new language has come to be applied to schools, as Len Barton and Mike Oliver (1992) argue, in their essay on educational segregation. Through such concepts as efficiency and cost-effectiveness, targets and performance indicators, competences and appraisal, schools have become pressurized places, seeing their task as being to market themselves. With the introduction of Local Management of Schools, open enrolment and opting out, competition has been intensified. A market-led system such as this can only increase the vulnerabilty of certain pupil groups, and justify demands for segregation.

Caught in the midst of these pressures, teachers struggle to make room for all their pupils, to accommodate every social identity. But where individual children or young people persistently disrupt classroom learning – disturbing other pupils, creating chaos, openly defying any kind of authority – exclusion may be the only final resort. Reluctant though they generally are to exclude troublesome children, teachers are, after all, there to teach. Closely accountable as they now are, there is little leeway for manoeuvre. Teaching is judged by its testable products. Those who cannot produce regular evidence of 'standards' run the risk of being themselves judged professionally inadequate.

In current exclusions from mainstream schooling, it is, of course, disruptive and aggressive children, children who present 'behavioural difficulties', who are particularly at issue. As many studies have now documented, such pupils are typically male and largely from lower socio-economic backgrounds; and Black children are greatly over-represented among them. These are pupils who do not 'fit in' to mainstream schooling, as it is generally organized.

During the period in which the Rampton Enquiry, later the Swann Report, came to be set up, there was widespread concern about what was defined as the underachievement of Black pupils. It was generally believed that, perhaps through the effects of father-absence, Black boys were failing to apply themselves to school learning, and hence falling short of their potential. But this view was strongly contested by many Black people. Through the consciousness-raising work of various pressure groups, the whole concept of Black underachievement came to be challenged.

In the common wisdom of the day, the mismatch between the schooling system and its Afro-Caribbean male pupils had been interpreted as deriving from personal inadequacies in the boys themselves. The problem was seen as located in individuals' motivational deficiencies. But in this new conceptual work, it came to be viewed quite differently; in essentially political terms. Redefined, the problem was one of cultural conflict, of a clash between the social values, assumptions and identities of the many people within the Black community and those of the mainstream community, affirmed in implicit and un-acknowledged ways in routine classroom practice.

Looked at in this way, the attribution of educational difference – whether framed as deviance and deficiency, or as special educational need – may act as a smokescreen hiding essentially political issues. So far from providing for the real, felt needs of those involved, such categorizations may instead serve the interests of dominant groups, by ensuring the perpetuation of their own particular norms and lifestyles, and at the same time disguising their failure to cater adequately for cultural minorities.

This conclusion seems to be borne out by the experience of those who come to be excluded from mainstream schooling. A decade ago I was involved in an investigation carried out by the Commission for Racial Equality (1985) into the use of suspension procedures within one local education authority. In the course of this investigation it became clear that, throughout the whole course of events, pupils and their parents felt generally unheard. Suspendees' own versions of the events leading to suspension were frequently not asked for at the hearings; if elicited, they were typically disregarded. The concerns of pupils and their parents about their future educational destinies were typically given equally short shrift.

A recent study into the exclusion of ethnic minority pupils (Bourne *et al.*, 1994) suggests that failure to acknowledge their own perspectives is still characteristic of these procedures. One such pupil whose case is documented was a Black girl whose attack on a White pupil followed the latter's racist abuse of her and her mother. The panel, which decided on permanent exclusion, took no account of how the incident was provoked.

Yet when schools do manage to make personal and cultural accommodation for their potentially troublesome pupils, their mutual relations are revolutionized. This is most clearly evident in contexts free from the pressure to teach a narrowly prescribed curriculum and to produce regular evidence of arbitrary standards. Many years ago, David Wills (1960) offered an account, based on his own practice, of how a special school might function as an educational milieu. Above all, he argued, disturbed and disturbing children need to feel a sense that the school belongs to them. By sharing, where legally and realistically possible, in decisions as to the running of the school, pupils experience participation and responsibility. They can legitimately claim the school as at least partly theirs. And on their side, school staff can affirm pupils' value as individuals: by taking pride in their endeavours, by showing that children are more important than furniture, by granting children's time a value equal to that of staff time.

Wills' vision is reflected, in many ways, in the recommendations of the Elton Report. This also stresses the importance of a sense of community and shared values. The need to respect pupils' own perspectives is emphasized in Elton's advocacy of open relationships, personal support and regular pastoral contacts. And there is a concern to avoid personal and cultural dissonance through the establishing and maintaining of the closest possible links with pupils' homes and communities.

It is clear that if schools are to meet their pupils on terms of greater justice, it is they which will have to make the larger accommodations. As things are now, many institutional traditions embody features which some pupils find inherently discriminatory and oppressive. The role demanded of young people, especially in the later years of schooling, is typically childish and demeaning, and runs counter to the maturity they have established in their out-of-school lives.

The flashpoint of this is often a confrontation over clothes. A petty insistence on regulation skirt lengths, a ban on Afro hairstyles or on trainers; such rules insult the adolescent pupils whose sense of identity is bound up in their adherence to particular fashions. Like clothing styles, ways of speaking are also personal, and can carry a kind of pride in oneself and one's social reference group. Official barring of dialect, of patois, of non-standard forms of English, is, however unintentionally, an affront. Of course many school rules are based on a real concern for pupils. But because their underlying reasons are seldom spelt out, they appear as arbitrary impositions of teacher power.

The official focus of children's engagement with schooling is that of classroom learning. In operating a public hierarchy of academic attainment, the present system ensures that some pupils will be losers. Being categorized as lower, being defined in terms of what one cannot do, carries an inevitable loss of personal status. Though teachers themselves characteristically look for strengths in their pupils, and seek, in David Hargreaves' phrase, to 'keep pupils clever', there are daily risks for unacademic children of classroom ridicule and humiliation.

As the visible representative of the whole educational establishment, it is teachers who must bear the brunt of pupils' resentments. And where classroom confrontations do arise, they typically carry features that lie outside the control of the particular teacher involved. In these situations, however, it is all too easy for both sides to set up the other as a cardboard cut-out: a caricature of lawlessness on the one side, of oppression on the other. Neither opponent acts alone. For the adolescent boy angrily confronting his teacher, the endorsement, the admiration of his watching classmates is crucial. To the teacher trying to contain the potential violence, at stake is his own professional reputation: the approval or the contemptuous pity of his colleagues. Both sides have to win. It has become necessary to fight to the death.

Hostility, in Kellyan psychology, is a desperate manoeuvre whereby we seek to evade the realities of a situation. Because so much of ourselves has been invested in achieving a particular outcome, we cannot allow the situation to appear as it really is, and so we try to cook the social books: to force it to appear differently. In typical classroom confrontations, both opponents may be doing this.

For the pupil, the predicament of having to give way is one he cannot accept. He must seize the situation and, by proving to himself and his classmates the hollowness of the teacher's authority, turn it into a personal victory. If for the teacher, the pupil's insolence and implicit violence can equally not be allowed, because they apparently threaten his competence as a teacher, the problem can only escalate. For it is only when, through the teacher's ability to step back from the confrontation, the situation becomes defused of its heavy personal investments, that a way out may be found.

Kelly's suggestion that we view hostility as a desperate attempt at self-protection urges us to abandon what he called 'the language of complaint'. Instead of focusing on the unpleasant effects which a particular action may have for others, it becomes necessary to step into the aggressor's shoes, to try to see what he or she may be attempting to achieve by such behaviour. Rather than seeing hostile behaviour as an in-built problem of particularly difficult individuals, it becomes possible to look for what is essentially at stake for young people who behave in this way. The situation may then be resolved, without either side 'winning', by means which allow pupils to keep face, to retain their vital sense of dignity.

The language of complaint; that is perhaps one way of defining the whole gamut of the terms that have been used to legitimize the poor educational treatment meted out to 'different' pupils. If we are to make more generous room within our schooling system, we need perhaps a Kellyan language, one which focuses on the perspectives, the personal subjectivities, of children themselves.

Chapter 8

Professional Learning

Masks have a way of sticking to our faces when worn too long. Verbs cease to express the invitational mood after the invitation has been accepted and experience has left its mark. To suggest to a person that he be what he has already become is not much of an invitation. ... Trouble sets in when [someone] begins to think that he really is a doctor, or a professor, or a scholar. When that happens he will have to spend most of his time making noises like doctors, professors or scholars, with the resultant failure from that time on to undertake anything interesting. He becomes trapped by verbs that have lapsed into the indicative mood when he wasn't looking.
(*Maher, 1969, pp. 158–9*)

Just back from two weeks in France with a group of third years, the French teacher sails into the staff room. Though she has taught for many years in this school, this is the first time she has taken the children abroad; the task has always before been delegated to a younger staff menber. To her colleagues she looks a different person. Previously tired, careworn, harassed, she now steps lightly, holds herself erect; there is a new freedom in all her movements. This woman who has always been too burdened, too preoccupied for anything more than urgent school business now positively bubbles over with enthusiasm.

The rough sea crossing, such an unpropitious start; how just like most of the children, she had been terribly sick, had had to defer the activities planned for the rest of the day. But how nice they had been about that. Her worries over the shyest, most isolated group member, and her surprised relief at the way some of the others had taken her under their wing. The evening sing-songs at the hostel breaking the ice among the various groups staying there, as well as bridging some linguistic gulfs. How returning one afternoon from a museum she had lost the way, and how, to her delighted astonishment, it was the most reluctant speaker of all who risked his French to question a passer-by. Above all, how mature and responsible the group had been throughout the whole trip, showing none of the objectionable behaviour for which they were so notorious in the classroom.

As this teacher announces to her colleagues – listening with weary envy to her unwonted exuberance – her own relationship with these pupils has been altogether transformed. Having got to know each other as individuals, there is a sense of mutual interest, liking and trust. Relations are now personal and intimate, rather than formal and authoritarian. It is impossible for them to revert to the way they were before.

For a few days, these confident anticipations seem to be borne out. The third-year pupils dwell on, mull over their experience with an equal enthusiasm and fascination. Like their teacher, they remark wonderingly on the transformation of their relationship. How different Miss was, she was really human, really nice. It was good to talk to her, she listened to you, she was interested. She wasn't like a teacher at all, she was just a person.

For a little while these feelings on both sides give an altogether different character to French lessons. But gradually another, more familiar atmosphere comes to dominate them – an atmosphere in which, in different ways, both teacher and pupils feel constrained, coerced. Neither side in the classroom relationship has wanted this to happen. Yet neither has been able to stop the gradual deterioration in their relationship. Somehow it has proved impossible to sustain, within the classroom, the mutual stance which each took up towards the other in the world beyond.

As human contexts, school classrooms are of course very different from those involved in accompanying children on a school trip. Where teachers are concerned, the classroom context is one of multiple heavy pressures, often crystallizing as constant pressure on *time*. Temporal tensions operate at every level. The difficult fifth-year group is at last getting interested and involved in the Pinter play they have been working on. But tomorrow you must leave that and begin a different text, keep up the relentless pace endemic in GCSE preparation. In another class, one child is obviously deeply troubled. But there is just no time to talk to her as you would like, alone, quietly and at length. You can only refer the child to the school pastoral system, and in the meantime, cope as best you can with the disruptive behaviour through which she regularly expresses distress.

For nearly all teachers the pressures felt to operate are not only those of time; there are also socio-political demands which press upon them and hem them in. Of all kinds of work, teaching has become subject to the most numerous, the most clamourous expressions of concern from other groupings. Probably in no other professional situation do so many different kinds of people feel such a strong and legitimate interest.

Parents, particularly in the primary phase, now bring increased pressures to bear. Employers, youth bodies, special interest groups, the community at large; all have their own vital investment in schooling. And more closely still, the influence of head teachers, heads of department and senior colleagues is felt, keenly if implicitly, by most teachers as they conduct their individual work. For all that classrooms are ostensibly private places where single teachers have their own unseen dealings with children, in reality most teachers bring with them a whole host of voices making loud and conflicting demands. If those who teach often express a sense of being beleaguered, this is hardly surprising.

More formally, universities and colleges, the educational establishment, Local Education Authorities, advisers and inspectors have always made their own authoritative demands on classroom business. But direct governmental intervention has hugely multiplied these pressures. Years after the passing of the Education Reform Act (1988), its consequences continue to impinge on teaching work. Implementation of management and pedagogic policies, of multiple and profound changes in curriculum content and assessment arrangements, has proved both lengthy and difficult. The professional adjustments made to accommodate these requirements have themselves been subjected to yet further revision, as ministerial policies constantly veer off in new directions. The rate of professional change currently demanded is surely unprecedented. Meanwhile new forms of accountability, in the OFSTED (Office for Standards in Education) inspection system, threaten those who fail adequately to update their classroom work.

Nor is it only adult groupings which, formally or informally, press their demands on teachers. Lively, active children and young people, who must spend their time as pupils, do not merely wait passively for what is to happen. They bring their own wills and expectations – their hopes and interests, their resentment, frustration, boredom or restlessness. The transactions, the activities of the classroom are, obviously, not just the creation of the teacher, but a product of constant, active negotiation between the often conflicting desires and intentions of teachers and pupils.

For many a teacher, the intensity of these moment-to-moment pressures – the sheer difficulty of staying in control of events, keeping one step ahead of 25 restless, ebullient young people – creates a sense of non-manoeuvrability, of having no breathing space at all. So far from feeling in charge of every initiative, teachers may experience themselves as just trying to respond adequately to those of their charges. They may see themselves, however regretfully, as essentially reactive rather than proactive in their work. Though you know that your handling of some regularly recurring problem is less than satisfactory, under the pressure of the moment you cannot help falling back into the old reactions.

Teaching entails, increasingly, a position which is questioned from all sides, a practice which is subject to contradictory pressures and incompatible demands. In the present political climate, teachers are held closely accountable and at the same time deprofessionalized. This situation is one which can lead, beyond mere stress, into powerlessness and alienation. Nominally in charge, teachers can easily feel a lack of personal autonomy. They may, in Kelly's term, suffer fragmentation: a disjunction between themselves and their own professional role. Their work may come to seem merely a part they are playing – a part having little resonance within their deepest feelings, their most significant hopes.

Yet the logic which applies to pupils applies to teachers too. Though certain difficult common denominators apply to nearly all practitioners, every teacher's situation is unique. Beyond the apparent uniformity of the teaching situation, each person constructs their own version of classroom reality, its meanings for the work they do there, its constraints and possibilities. And just as the perspectives of pupils need to be understood, so it is vitally important to acknowledge the personal subjectivities of those who teach.

In an unusual study conducted some years ago, Anthony Rosie (1979) closely explored the subjective positions of three colleagues in the English department of an outer London comprehensive. As a member of their department, Rosie had established a remarkable level of trust on the part of his colleagues, who spoke to him very openly. Their situation was in fact fraught with professional difficulty and tension.

Here is Rosie's sketch of the three teachers involved:

Jeff. Jeff was now the new Head of Department. Aged 32, he had taught in a number of schools and was keen to develop mixed-ability teaching and a language policy as it was envisaged in the Bullock Report (1975).
Stephen. Stephen was in charge of the internal examinations and some of the public examinations. Aged 47, he had taught at the school for ten years, having taught in a variety of other schools.
Jean. Jean was in charge of Drama teaching. Aged 33, she had taught at the school for four years after training as a mature student. This was the only school where she had taught.
(*Rosie, 1979, pp. 328–9*)

During the year in which Jeff has been head of department, both Stephen and Jean have come to experience his position as diametrically opposite to their own. So impossible does this situation seem that each is contemplating resignation. Rosie examines the constructions which have led to such drastic solutions. As part of an independent research project, all three teachers have completed a questionnaire. This invites them to judge the importance for pupils of the following dimensions:

1 being quiet and orderly;
2 not interrupting the teacher when he or she is speaking;
3 wearing school uniform;
4 doing homework;
5 paying attention in class;
6 keeping up with the work;
7 learning to work on your own.

Both Stephen and Jean strongly endorse the importance of all these dimensions. Jeff, on the other hand, argues that other dimensions are more important: particularly those that promote classroom conversation. But it is in their elaboration of these dimensions of meaning that the different constructions of these three teachers becomes evident.

Rosie's exploration of personal construing demanded that teachers redefined the questionnaire dimensions. The three teachers were asked to say, for each dimension, what would be its opposite, and

then, what would be the opposite of that. This rather oblique operation produced a more personal reading of the questionnaire. For
four dimensions, Stephen and Jean share interpretations that stand in
marked contrast to those of Jeff:

Original	Stephen	Jean	Jeff
Not interrupting the teacher.	Being courteous.	Being well behaved.	Being interested in the lesson.
Paying attention in class.	Getting on with work.	Getting on with work.	Finding it necessary to listen.
Keeping up with the work.	Capable of doing the work.	Able to do the work without trouble.	Finding the work interesting.
Learning to work on your own.	Working on your own.	Becoming independent.	Discovering that teachers don't know everything.

These alternative slants on the same starting points illustrate two very
different teaching orientations. On their side, Stephen and Jean speak
from positions close to the original dimensions; emphasizing the
importance of order in the classroom, of quietness and good behaviour, of attention to teacher instruction. For Jeff, on the other hand,
recognition of pupils' perspectives is vital; he speaks from a position
which affirms the importance of children's active engagement in
classroom work. Such differences do indeed, as Rosie suggests, seem
profound.

On this evidence, Jean and Stephen share very similar outlooks.
Yet in fact they are quite diverse. Though both emphasize good
behaviour, this is from different standpoints. For Jean, it means
caring and supportive relationships. It is in these terms, too, that she
defines her present situation as intolerable: 'No one seems to spend
time on people here and there's no caring. It's the little things that
matter.... At first I thought Jeff was a welcome relief.... But he never
remembered what it was like for me to teach eight periods of Drama a
day' (Rosie, 1979, p. 333).

For Stephen good behaviour on the part of pupils is crucial too, but
carries rather different connotations: 'I insist on order in the class-

room and I won't have children disobeying me. They must learn that I'm in authority' (Rosie, 1979, p. 334). Stephen views teaching as establishing a status which confers certain duties and powers. It is teachers' reponsibility to demand order, and to make judgements of pupils that should not be called into question. This is the sphere where Stephen's relations with Jeff are particularly problematic: 'He believes in mixed ability but of course it doesn't work. I don't agree with his ideas.... Take this new business of not marking every mistake and not giving a numerical mark for younger children. It annoys me, It goes against everything I believe in' (Rosie, 1979, p. 334).

How does Jeff, the head of department, see things? Jeff is aware of serious problems in his department:

> I know there's a rift between Stephen, Jean and myself. For Stephen I think the fact that he is the oldest person in the department and has always believed in rules has formed his outlook. He is not sympathetic to the needs of children, He works hard according to his lights but it's lists and rules, no thinking.
> (*Rosie, 1979, p. 335*)

It seems that between these two teachers, little sociality exists; neither has achieved an appreciative understanding of the other's outlook. Both have failed to enter imaginatively into the other's subjective world, to step provisionally into their colleague's shoes. In their different ways, both Jeff and Stephen write off the other's approach to teaching. In relation to Jean and Jeff, the situation is no better. On her side, Jean sees Jeff as essentially uncaring. Aware that Jean feels troubled, Jeff fails to recognize her sense of being unsupported in her teaching, and instead defines her as a problematic person: 'I think Jean needs help. She is obviously under strain but she doesn't respond too well. I don't think her problems are necessarily school-based but she is beginning to cause trouble' (Rosie, 1979, p. 335).

This case study shows three teachers badly at odds with each other. For each, the positions of their colleagues are of real moment. No classroom is an island. In individual dealings with pupils, every teacher is likely to be keenly aware of support or challenge from professional colleagues. Where one's particular ethos is totally at variance with that of the school, the head or head of department, the classroom seems permeated, invaded by another frame of reference – alien, hostile, threatening. In situations such as these, resort to resignation may appear the only possible solution.

Such extreme dissension among close colleagues is, fortunately, rare. Yet many teachers experience, if not actual hostility, a general sense of professional isolation and lack of support. The teaching situation is one in which sociality is not easily developed. For all the numberless meetings – departmental, house, whole school, with parents, formal or informal, regular or crisis – there are likely to be few occasions on which it is possible to talk with colleagues openly, freely and at length. Sometimes this is through the presence of those higher in the hierarchy – people who could block promotion prospects, or prohibit change.

But there are also other, less overt threats to teachers' freedom of expression and the genuine sharing of experience, factors making for a necessary personal guardedness. As Guy Claxton (1993) has argued, every staff room has its own tacit rules, defining what is collectively thought of as normal teacher behaviour. Stepping beyond these bounds means risking being seen as odd or inept.

Departures from normative practice, failures to maintain 'proper order' may need to be kept secret. And there is, almost universally, a conspiracy of silence on the topic of personal doubts and difficulties in teaching. While staff room cultures allow certain pupils, or groups of pupils, to be defined as deviant, problematic or objectionable, they absolutely forbid the confession of one's own sense of failure, conflict or despair. Teachers' real problems, if voiced at all, are usually bypassed or trivialized by ritual humour.

All this makes professional development extremely difficult. One consequence of the taboo on expressing difficulties is that it inhibits personal awareness. Without being able to articulate our own constructions – the basic assumptions from which we act – we cannot begin to reflect on our own practices. Such reflection, impossible while immersed in classroom business, is vital when things go regularly wrong. Unless you can consider the situation in depth and at some distance – see what is actually going on, envisage other possible avenues of approach, imagine how these might turn out – you can never hope to escape the same old vicious circle.

Faced, for the umpteenth time, with the growing uproar of a bored and restless class on a sweltering Friday afternoon, yet again you find yourself shouting. You can hear yourself beginning to lose your self-control; you know the children sense it too. This is no way to restore calm and sanity, it can only result in an escalation of disorder and violence. But you are dog-tired at the end of a heavy week, it is only three weeks into the term, and you have a full schedule of marking and preparation filling the weekend ahead. You must at all costs stop this unruly, uproarious behaviour; what else *is* there to do?

Trapped in classroom situations that feel like prisons, many teachers long for change. And on the face of it, their profession enjoys a superabundance of developmental opportunities. In the avalanche of directives that has descended on shcools over the last few years, teachers are invited almost weekly to try out new approaches. But these invitations are typically hollow. This is not only because they may be mutually contradictory, or even because they often have no clear rationale. More fundamentally, to the extent that these initiatives are imposed from outside the teaching profession itself, they remain ungrounded in classroom realities. As such, they lack credibility for teachers.

No less than beginning teachers, most experienced practitioners aspire to develop their own professional practice. But this kind of learning can proceed only out of real practical concerns, directly relevant classroom issues. It lies a world away from the top-down, often arbitrary changes in practice to which teachers have become all too accustomed.

Very different from politically inspired demands for change, initiatives in teaching have often come from within the profession itself. Until recently, this has been particularly true of new departures in the curriculum, where the proposals offered by specialized professional groupings have been mediated through advisory work. By supporting long term group work, and ownership of change on the part of the teachers involved, such initiatives have often achieved significant breakthroughs in attitudes and practice. This way of organizing development has, however, been virtually phased out, and replaced by bought-in INSET (in-service training) support. All too often this format lacks opportunities for long term collaborative work. As a result, the desired change fails to happen.

In a discussion of professional development, Colin Biott (1992) suggests that there is frequently a lack of clarity in the introduction of new initiatives, a failure to define precisely what is being aimed at. But more often, he believes, the innovation falls short because of the artificial circumstances in which change has been conceived. If new materials, new modes, are to be adopted, they must prove viable within the complex human contexts in which teachers actually work. Every classroom, as Kelly would insist, has its own system of commonality and sociality, its own unique cultural world. Alterations in practice cannot be arbitrarily introduced; they must make sense to those involved.

Any attempt to facilitate professional development has, most basically, to build in time for teachers to reflect on their own practice. With the additional demands now made by the National Curriculum, many teachers feel they are forever on the run, with no opportunity to stand still and take stock of their own work. Nor, of course, can professional change occur through innovations that ignore subjective realities. When development does occur, it is through work which addresses teachers' real questions, which speaks to their felt predicaments, which offers strategies that seem both feasible and worthwhile. These are principles that guide many induction schemes.

In the role of mentor, a senior staff member works with a newly qualified teacher. In protected time and space, they mull things over together: discussing the last lesson, its successes and its difficulties, considering other possible ways of working and what these might entail, envisaging and planning the next lesson. With the support and encouragement of a sympathetic and experienced colleague, new teachers can reflect at length on their own practice. This allows a growing appreciation of personal strengths and weaknesses, within an essentially supportive rather than judgemental context. Aims and strategies take on a sharper focus; it becomes possible to try out new perspectives, experiment with different approaches.

But it is not only new teachers who characteristically benefit from these opportunities for shared reflection. For those who take the role of mentor, these occasions often act as a catalyst in their own professional development. Close consideration of a colleague's teaching tends to raise fundamental issues that apply equally in one's own work. Such beneficial collaboration does of course depend on institutional support. At a time when many schools are facing budgetary cuts, this calls for real commitment to professional development.

In mentoring, at its best, the perspectives of those involved are acknowledged and accorded professional respect. This means, essentially, a situation of partnership and collaboration. Dealings based on power and status differentials kill such development. Facilitative contexts are those that allow 'tutors' and 'students' to work together. Brought to bear on shared concerns, their different perspectives, different spheres of experience and understanding can produce approaches that are new to both.

Exactly the same principles underlie good practice in the operation of appraisal schemes. If managed in this way, appraisal can prove genuinely constructive. As a collaborative undertaking, it may represent a helpful occasion for a comprehensive professional review. The equality of the relationship ensures that discussion takes place within the teacher's own frame of reference, and that potential ways forward are sensitively negotiated. Potentially, appraisal schemes offer what Christopher Day (1993, p. 17) calls 'critical friendships'. However, this is clearly not always achieved. The managerial context may instead constrain the appraisee to 'play it safe', rather than take professional risks in displaying what may appear as personal inadequacies and failures.

Professional learning probably always takes place in contexts of collaboration. Where general teaching concerns are debated with colleagues, strategies can be worked out that are collectively agreed and endorsed. In some school settings head teachers inspire collective visions and support collaborative work. And when policies are genuinely whole school, when team teaching is routine, when teachers feel comfortable with the presence of a colleague in their classroom – then it becomes natural to evolve joint strategies for change. But there are also schools that are run on authoritarian lines. There, staff may find few opportunities to contribute to policy. Efforts at collaborative innovation may be heavily discouraged. Such personal isolation and lack of solidarity are inimical to professional development.

Of all learning contexts, teachers' own research initiatives are perhaps the most fertile. Brought together by some shared professional concern, members of these groupings closely debate problems and strategies, compare notes and exchange good practice. The investigation to address unresolved issues grows directly out of this discussion. It sets out to gather evidence which, for those involved, will have real bearing on their own questions. It is conducted by teachers themselves, and they interpret what the outcomes mean. Such undertakings, initiated and controlled at every stage by those concerned, can provide new understandings that 'belong' to teachers, and are anchored in the real life contexts of schools and classrooms.

Possibilities for change that arise out of teachers' own research activities are likely, subjectively, to carry credibility for individual practitioners. Yet even with the support of an ongoing group, actually changing one's practice remains a difficult act. It is one thing to learn of a colleague's successful approach to a shared problem, but quite another to take it on board yourself. Just as for pupils testing out new knowledge, teachers have to feel that a different way of working can be squared with their own personal and professional identity.

One evening, in your teachers' research group, you discuss the problem of second language learners. This is a problem which, as you are all too well aware, you have not even begun to resolve. A fellow teacher, with enthusiasm and conviction, describes how he approaches things: enlisting parents to translate worksheets, bringing in second language speakers, setting up games in which indigenous children have to learn from their Bangladeshi classmates. This is working very well for him; why not, as he asks encouragingly, try it yourself? You can only agree that strategies like these might produce equal breakthroughs in your own classroom.

Yet somehow, the prospect of actually adopting these approaches is not straightforward. It is all very well for your colleague, but you are not really that sort of teacher. Your dealings with parents and the community have never been casual or informal. Opening up your lessons to people from outside would be a major departure from the teaching approach you have always taken. And what would happen if you were to introduce games into your classroom? Might not things degenerate into a situation you could not control? Nor, it seems, could you even begin to try all this without a loss of general credibility. Wherever you have taught, the children have always seen you as a formal teacher, strict but fair, who takes her classroom work seriously. To your colleagues, too, you are known as someone who stands for traditional values, who insists in her teaching on the basic importance of order, respect, authority.

New ways of working professionally must be delicately negotiated. Some teaching strategies may prove in the end irreconcilable with particular teacher identities. But every possible new departure has at first to be tried out provisionally, imaginatively anticipated for what it might entail. In the same way that pupils need a kind of protected space for different ways of thinking, teachers need a freedom from their usual professional responsibility; a context in which they can think about potential change at a distance, without as yet having to own it. In this, the forum of a research group can often prove facilitative. Removed from the pressures of classroom business, involving colleagues from a wide diversity of professional placements and concerns, this arena allows freedom for exploratory thinking – shared and supported ventures into the professional unknown.

References

Bannister, D. and Fransella, F. (1986) *Inquiring Man: The Psychology of Personal Constructs.* London: Croom Helm.

Barnes, D. 'Language in the secondary classroom', in D. Barnes, J. Britton and M. Torbe, (1986) *Language, the Learner and the School.* Harmonsworth: Penguin.

Barton, L. and Oliver, M. (1992) 'Special needs: personal trouble or public issue?', in M. Arnot and L. Barton (eds) *Voicing Concerns: Sociological Perspectives on Contemporary Educational Reforms.* Wallingford: Triangle Books Ltd.

Biott, C. (1992) 'Imposed support for teachers' learning: implementation or development partnerships?', in C. Biott and J. Nias (eds) *Working and Learning Together for Change.* Buckingham and Philadelphia: Open University Press.

Bourne, J., Bridge, L. and Searle, C. (1994) *Outcast England: How Schools Exclude Black Children.* London: Institute of Race Relations.

Bruner, J. (1990) *Acts of Meaning.* Cambridge, Mass. and London: Harvard University Press.

Claxton, G. (1984) *Live and Learn: An Introduction to the Psychology of Growth and Change.* Cambridge and New York: Harper & Row.

Claxton, G. (1993) *Being a Teacher: A Positive Approach to Change and Stress.* London: Cassell.

Cohen, P. (1987) 'Racism and popular culture', *Working Paper 9.* London: University Centre for Multi-Cultural Education.

Cohen, P. (1988) 'The perversions of inheritance', in P. Cohen and H. S. Baines (eds) *Multi-Racist Britain.* Basingstoke: Macmillan.

Commission for Racial Equality (1985) *Birmingham Local Education Authority: Referral and Suspension of Pupils.* London: Commission for Racial Equality.

Commission for Racial Equality (1987) *Learning in Terror.* London: Commission for Racial Equality.

Cooper, P., Smith, C. J. and Upton, G. (1994) *Emotional and Behavioural Difficulties.* London and New York: Routledge.

Day, C. (1993) 'Reflection: a necessary but not sufficient condition for professional development', *British Educational Research Journal*, 19(1), 83–93.

DES (1992) *The National Curriculum.* London: HMSO.

Donaldson, M. (1978) *Children's Minds.* London: Fontana.

Eliot, J. (1991) 'Human values: a critique of National Curriculum development', *Curriculum Journal*, 2, 1.

Furlong, J. (1992) 'Reconstructing professionalism: ideological struggle in initial teacher education', in M. Arnot and L. Barton (eds) *Voicing Concerns: Sociological Perspectives on Contemporary Educational Reforms.* Oxford: Triangle Books Ltd.

Gardner, H. and Perkins, D. N. (eds) (1989) *Art, Mind and Education: Research from Project Zero.* Cambridge, Mass.: Harvard University Press.

Hargreaves, D. J. (1977) 'Sex roles in divergent thinking', *British Journal of Educational Psychology*, 47, 26–32.

Hargreaves, D. H., Hester, S. K. and Mellor, F. J. (1975) *Deviance in Classrooms.* London: Routledge and Kegan Paul.

Harri-Augstein, S. and Thomas, L. (1991) *Learning Conversations.* London and New York: Routledge.

Hartley, R. (1986) 'Imagine you're clever', *Journal of Child Psychology and Psychiatry* 27, 3, 383–98.

Heisenberg, W. (1958) *Physics and Philosophy.* New York: Harper Row.

Huggett, F. E. (1986) *Teachers.* London: Weidenfeld and Nicolson.

Hughes, M., Wikely, F. and Nash, T (1993) *Parents and their Children's Schools.* London: Blackwell.

Jackson, P. W. (1968) *Life in Classrooms.* Cambridge, Mass.: Holt, Rinehart and Winston.

Kelly, G. A. (1955) *The Psychology of Personal Constructs.* New York: Norton.

Kelly, G. A. (1978) 'The psychology of aggression' in Fransella, F. (ed.) *Personal Construct Psychology 1977*, London: Academic Press.

Kohl, H. (1971) *36 Children.* Harmondsworth: Penguin.

Lee, L. (1965) *Cider with Rosie.* London: Hogarth Press.

Maher, B. (ed.) (1969) *Clinical Psychology and Personality: The Selected Papers of George Kelly.* New York and London: John Wiley and Sons.

Phillips, E. M. (1982) 'Developing by design', *Vocational Aspects of Education*, 34, 31–6.

Pope, M. and Keen, T. (1981) *Personal Construct Theory and Education*, London and New York: Academic Press.

Potts, P. (1984) *Integrating Pre-school with Special Needs.* London: Centre for Studies on Integration in Education.

Rich, A. (1989) 'Invisibility in academe', quoted by R. Rosaldo in *Culture and Truth: The Remaking of Social Analysis.* Boston: Beacon Press.

Rogers, C. (1983) *Freedom to Learn for the 80s.* Boston: Charles Merrill Publishing Company.

Rosen, H. (1993) *Troublesome Boy.* London: English and Media Centre, Institute of Education.

Rosie, A. J. (1979) 'Teachers and children: interpersonal relations in the classroom', in P. Stringer and D. Bannister (eds) *Constructions of Sociality and Individuality*. London and New York: Academic Press.

Runkel, P. J. and Damrin, D. E. (1961) 'The effect of training and anxiety upon teachers' preferences for information about students', *Educational Psychology*, **52**, 254–61.

Ryan, J. and Thomas, D. (1980) *The Politics of Mental Handicap*. Harmondsworth: Penguin.

Said, E. (1993) *Representations of the Intellectual* (Reith Lectures) London: BBC Publications.

Salmon, P. and Claire, H. (1984) *Classroom Collaboration*. London: Routledge and Kegan Paul.

Skidelsky, K. (1994) quoted in M. Bassey, 'Why Lord Skidelsky is so wrong', *Times Educational Supplement*, 21 January 1994.

Smith, L. (1988) *Dimensions of Childhood: A Handbook for Social Education at 16+*. London: UNICEF (UK) and Health Education Authority.

Tizard, B. and Hughes, M. (1984) *Young Children Learning*. London: Fontana.

van Allen, I. (1994) 'The hidden scars of war', *Times Educational Supplement*, 25 February 1994.

Walden, R. and Walkerdine, V. (1985) 'Girls and mathematics: from primary to secondary schooling', (Bedford Way Papers No. 9), London: Institute of Education.

Walkerdine, V. and Lucey, H. (1989) *Democracy in the Kitchen: Regulating Mothers and Socialising Daughters*. London: Virago.

Willes, M. (1983) *Children into Pupils*. London: Routledge and Kegan Paul.

Willis, P. (1977) *Learning to Labour*. Farnborough: Saxon House.

Willis, D. (1960) *Throw Away Thy Rod*. London: Victor Gollancz.

Woodhead, M. (1993) 'Psychology and the cultural construction of children's needs', in A. James and A. Prout (eds) *Constructing and Reconstructing Childhood*. London: Falmer Press.

Wright, C. (1992) *Race Relations in the Primary School*. London: Fulton.

Index